jump

Daniella Moyles is an Irish model, presenter and travel writer. Beginning her career aged 18, she worked primarily as a model before transitioning to television and radio presenting. In 2017 she left that career behind to backpack around the globe for two years. She is currently undertaking a degree to become a psychotherapist and is the founder of STLL, a holistic-living and wellness business.

jump

ONE GIRL'S SEARCH FOR MEANING

DANIELLA MOYLES

Gill Books

Gill Books
Hume Avenue
Park West
Dublin 12
www.gillbooks.ie
Gill Books is an imprint of M.H. Gill and Co.

978 07171 8672 3

Designed by Marsha Swan
Edited by Emma Dunne
Proofread by Kristin Jensen
Printed by ScandBook in Lithuania
This book is typeset in Sabon

The paper used in this book comes from the wood pulp of managed forests. For every tree felled, at least one tree is planted, thereby renewing natural resources.

A CIP catalogue record for this book is available from the British Library.

5 4 3 2 1

For my dad, the most courageous and authentic person I know. I love you.

contents

PART ONE

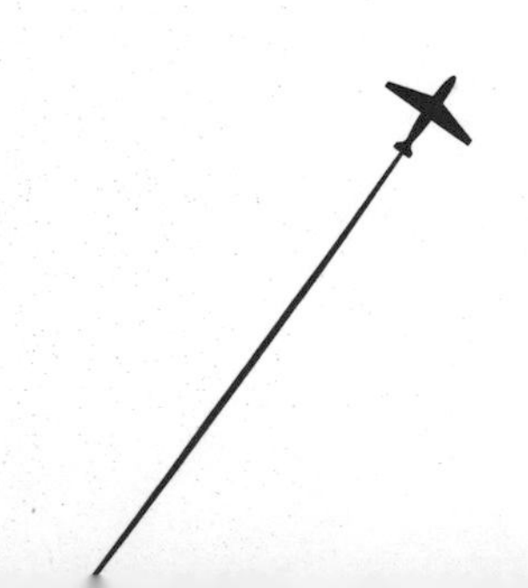

PART TWO

prologue

The rain is hammering on the windscreen. I have my wipers set to the highest speed. I can't decide if it's their inability to clear the droplets fast enough that's blurring my vision or if it's that undeniable sense of dread creeping up my spine. *Stop*, I tell myself, *you are fine*. I blink, roll my head slightly left to right and try desperately to focus on the road. It doesn't work. Everything's beginning to feel dangerous and chaotic. Cars pass in a speeding flash of splash and colour. The hum of unidentifiable sounds coming from my radio is too loud – I should turn that down. I reach for the volume knob, but my shaking hand and blurred vision make this simple act unrecognisably challenging. The obvious loss of control over my body only serves to worsen the panic building in my head and chest. My heart pounds; beads of sweat line my upper lip on this cold, grey afternoon. I grasp the steering wheel tightly and brake for a sense of control. I am surely driving much too slowly on the motorway. My boyfriend, sitting in the passenger seat, will notice, ask what's wrong and then this will all be real. He says something I don't fully register, but judging from his tone he seems unaware of my gradual internal collapse. A delayed and vague 'yeah' weakly escapes from my mouth, so dry my tongue can barely enunciate this simple monosyllable. Thankfully, it seems to serve as a reasonable response to whatever he's said. He will attribute my bizarre demeanour to a terrible hang-over, I reason. Still, I cannot focus my vision. I cannot settle the growing feeling of terror now forcefully encouraging me to spontaneously empty my bowels in the driving seat of my car while I try to maintain a rapidly decaying façade of normalcy. I stir uncomfortably as my abdomen pangs with those familiar cramps I have self-diagnosed as IBS, an ailment of elusive origin and endless ineffective treatment options I have been obsessing over for months. This is the least intimidating symptom of my accelerating emotional state and I happily allow it to distract me momentarily, pondering if I'd eaten some dairy, eggs, gluten or other recently diagnosed intolerance during last night's dinner. And then it starts, the frightening big finale, in spite of my every desperate attempt to resist it. Blurred vision morphs into a rapidly receding dark tunnel. My thoughts, already foggy and unbearably slow, begin to detach from reality. My coherent picture of the world, my sense of self and my place in it, every retrievable memory, everything I know to be real and true – it all cuts loose from the roots that bind me to logic and reason, floating like a muddy soup in my mind. An eardrum-bursting scream is trapped in my heavy chest but I'm frozen, petrified. I don't remember doing it but I have stopped the car – my internal state has clearly spilled over into something undeniably physical, judging by the wide-eyed, ashen look on the suddenly unfamiliar face of the man beside me.

His expression, a mixture of pure bewilderment and concern, only fans the flames of my terror. I am convinced there is no salvation from this place. I am still breathing but I am gone. On the thin, wavering edge of an abyss I feebly try to explain, 'I don't know who or where I am.'

∘ ∘ ∘

This day changed my life.

It derailed almost everything I had worked to achieve up to that point and set me, willing or not, on a new path with no signposts and a barely visible track. It forced me to stop, take a long overdue, sincere self-assessment and ultimately start over in ways I never could have imagined I was capable of. It taught me that our greatest anguish is always the doorway to our most significant lessons and opportunities for growth. That resisting what is will only ever lead to misery, pain and complete misalignment in your life. It led me kicking and screaming to absolute, undeniable authenticity and self-love. It was a glorious gift, wrapped like an onion in the thickest skin, and peeling back those layers is the purpose of this book.

But before we delve into the darkest corners of my human experience, I should probably introduce myself and explain how I ended up here.

PART ONE

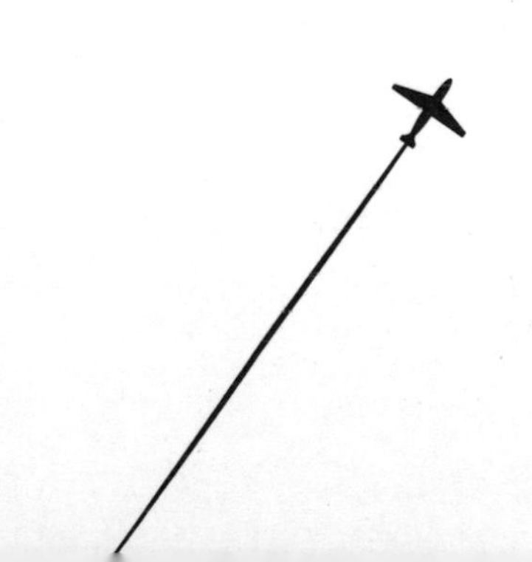

CHAPTER 1

childhood

'No mud, no lotus'

THICH NHAT HANH

My name is Daniella – such an exotic choice in 1980s Ireland that my granny could only remember it when she rhymed it with the over-the-counter mouth-ulcer gel Bonjela. Personally, I never minded the misleading Latina connotations; instead I take issue with the number of syllables necessary to pronounce it, which results in 99.9 per cent of people giving up listening halfway through and calling me 'Danielle' forever more. Still, my mother (who has yet to visit any part of Latin America) makes no apologies for it. Probably because day to day my close friends and family just call me Dell, like the computer, which is much easier to contend with.

I grew up in a copy-and-paste middle-class housing estate on the rural outskirts of the commuter town of Naas in County Kildare, an equestrian hub of midlands Ireland. Naas is a must-visit for any mother-of-the-bride on the hunt for a headpiece, as well as being somewhat infamous throughout the country for hosting the annual three-day rain-soaked music festival Witness, later renamed Oxegen, in one of the nearby racecourses.

Once a year, thousands of festivalgoers would descend on our tiny main street and seriously challenge the town council's latest inadequate attempt at crowd control and additional infrastructure. My mother would complain for three days solid that she couldn't get near Tesco, and even when she managed to surmount the mobs with perseverance and brute force, the shelves were as empty as the end of days. This is truly any Irish mother's living nightmare, so my childhood associations with the most exciting carnival to pass through our small community were distasteful to say the least. That, coupled with my having zero exposure to horses, little interest in French lace and a strict curfew, made Naas an entirely uneventful place to grow up.

We did, however, have a local McDonald's, a very thrilling, modern claim for any 1990s provincial town, and I do remember the ribbon-cutting opening ceremony vividly. It was a big day for the parish, but not for me. I was born with a preference for vegetables; my favourite food growing up was Brussels sprouts, which, strangely, were nowhere to be found on a McDonald's menu.

My parents moved to Naas the year before I was born because Dad got a job as head chef in the restaurant of a hotel in the heart of the main street. I would sometimes pop across to him for an egg mayonnaise sandwich on my school break. I attended a Catholic all-girls public school and until my teenage years was a quiet, obedient student. Most of my youthful energy came from a penchant for performance, and one of the ways I would channel that was altar serving at the school's adjoining church. I should explain: altar serving was never a dream of mine – I had wanted to be a ballerina. My mam bought me a blue leotard, a matching blue ballet skirt, nude tights and soft ballet pumps. I remember feeling I really looked the part when I was enrolled for classes that were to take place weekly in the conservatory at the back of some lady's house. I was surely on a direct course to the *Nutcracker*. But as fate would have it, I took just three lessons before the town's only teacher decided to relocate, taking my budding ballerina dreams with her. I did speech and drama and hip-hop dance classes after that, but the work-to-performance ratio was unrewarding for me. Two end-of-year shows just weren't satiating enough. I could altar serve multiple days a week and get to feel like I was on stage, especially when I was regularly bestowed with the honour of ringing the bells during the blessing of the bread. I liked the elaborate dress, the familiar choreographed flow of a sermon and the challenge to never break character as the most solemn, angelic nine-year-old you had ever laid eyes on. I never listened to a word the priests said – in my mind, this was a one-person show and all eyes in the congregation were on me.

But mainly I liked to altar serve because it made my dad happy. He was born somewhere in the middle of 14 siblings, a family of 16 in total, raised in a very small cottage in Bantiss, County Tipperary, to a labourer father and an exceptional mother. Now, as a 30-year-old mother of none, the strength of my female lineage never ceases to amaze me. The Catholic Church ruled strong across the country then, religion was forcefully instilled and contraception was clearly evil. My dad left his home and his school, run by priests who taught with beatings, aged just 13 to work in hotel kitchens for food and board. It was the early 1970s and even at that tender age, considering his circumstances and his potential future, he knew this was his wisest option and never looked back. When we were young he worked a lot, so much that we rarely saw him. But I knew he was still very religious, as Sunday mass was a non-negotiable weekly family affair. I thought altar serving would make him proud of me. For his extra approval, I would sometimes get up and cycle in to town to serve the 6 a.m. mass before school. And this approval-seeking behaviour had its perks: it was unsurprisingly perceived as an admirable level of commitment to the role, so I was often bumped up the roster of choice for the paid gigs – weddings and funerals – after which I would receive a fiver in an envelope and proceed to buy a 50p bag of chips in the chipper across the road. I believe this is called reward conditioning. As a spiritual atheist now, I blame this rewiring of my neural circuitry for my prolonged positive associations with the Church. My dad, now a spiritual atheist also, would use this claim as grounds to question the foundation of the school of behaviourism, as his conditioning was most definitely far from rewarding.

His religious upbringing was also not quite strong enough to dissuade him from the evils of contraception, as I am the eldest of just two. My brother, Richard, is four years younger but twenty years wiser than me since the day he arrived. He is the most wonderful human being I could ever wish to be immediately related to, and I adore him with every cell of my body. He is also my polar opposite, for which I am very grateful, because it gives our mother one stable, well-adjusted child. I am wildly impulsive and unpredictable, driven mostly by novelty. He is a homebody who values routine and familiarity. My emotional maturity was hard earned, at a cost to others and myself, and is still evolving. It seems to me he was simply born innately compassionate, wholly empathetic and impressively self-aware.

He completed his degree in computer programming straight out of school. After school I took a year out, then decided to go to art college, dropped out within the first year, took another year or two out and then went back to university to study psychology and, again, dropped out. I'm 30, unemployed by conventional standards, single and currently writing this sentence in a hostel in Perth. He is 26, an asset to his company, engaged and living in his own beautiful flat, complete with two pet bunnies, overlooking a picture-perfect canal in a small village just 15 minutes' drive from my parents' house. I am chalk and he is cheese, and everybody likes cheese.

Despite our obvious differences, we are both technically miracles. My mam, who had me aged just 23, was told her liver would struggle to support a healthy pregnancy. Based on this, I like to think my opposition to conformity began in the womb. I was born six weeks early with a lovely jaundice glow, finally relieving my poor mother of living with crippling cholestasis, a condition caused by liver disease that results in severe and constant itching all over the body while tripling the risk of a stillbirth.

I spent much of my young life watching my mam battle various health issues – she was the last of eight children in her family and I'm convinced her parents had just run out of all the good stuff when it came to making her. For years on end,

I would find her bent over, heaving into a basin and groaning in pain. She suffered from constantly recurring gallstones that ultimately nearly killed her. During one of her many keyhole surgeries to remove them from her abdomen, she had a severe allergic reaction to the dye that was pumped into her blood to highlight them. Her immune system was so compromised that she ended up in the intensive care unit fighting life-threatening pancreatitis and other complications simultaneously for months after. My brother and I were shipped around from relatives to neighbours while my dad tried to keep everything afloat, juggling work, school runs and minding us and our mother. She was in the hospital in Dublin, an hour's drive away on a good day, so we didn't get to see her often. I remember she was just well enough to be allowed out for Christmas Day at home – trying to hide my shock and devastation at the sight of her feeble, sickly frame is all that's stayed with me from that day.

Thankfully, we eventually got her back and to full health, but far too soon after, I came home one evening from a friend's house to find her in anaphylactic shock, on one of the few nights my dad has probably ever left her side. For weeks prior she had been suffering from relentless allergic reactions to something entirely mysterious. One day her hand would swell to a comedic size, the next day her cheek, then the side of her neck. But now it was the inside of her throat. As I climbed the stairs I could hear her calling for me, a laboured, croaky whisper. My sympathetic nervous system kicked into gear with the good old fight-or-flight response – I knew immediately that something was very wrong. Still, I could not bring myself to turn on her bedroom light, too petrified of what was to greet me. But even in her state of distress, with time ticking rapidly against her, she managed to calm me, get me to turn the light on and explain what needed to happen.

My memory seems to completely black out when I try to recall situations of extreme stress – I know an ambulance arrived and she was almost intubated via an opening in her throat below the swelling, but I don't remember calling the emergency services or if I stayed with her when they arrived. I do know from stories she has told me since that she managed to convince them over the blare of the siren to give her 60 seconds after they administered the steroids to stop the swelling before they made the incision. She wanted the least traumatic series of events to play out and an intubation would mean days of hospitalisation, whereas the swelling beginning to subside would mean she could simply go home. She won that battle and was discharged the following morning after some tests – to this day we still don't know what caused that slew of reactions.

You'd be forgiven for thinking that must have been the end of her misfortunes, but it was only the warm-up act. I was 15 when she told me she had cancer. She was just 38. A lump in her breast had spread to the lymph nodes below her arm and maybe further. What I remember from the following year and a half is patchy at best. One scene that remains vividly etched into my mind is of her sitting rigidly upright in her hospital bed after a second tumour-removal operation: she was enclosed in a tight back brace and vomiting violently into a bucket; I asked if I could leave, get a tram into town and do some shopping. This period of my life brings me to my first dance with mental health and its powerful effects on behaviour. I had no control over my mam's illness or her potential survival, of course, but somewhere in my young, overwhelmed mind, I convinced myself that if I acted like she wasn't sick, maybe that would make it true. And so I embodied this thought entirely.

On the night she told me about her diagnosis, I went with my teenage boyfriend to see Tommy Tiernan perform his latest stand-up show. I remember leaving it wondering why I was the only one not laughing. My dad was very mad at me for going – 'You didn't have to celebrate it,' he told me – but it didn't register. Not one person in my school knew my mam was sick until nearly a year into her treatment. I point blank did not speak about it. When I visited her I was aloof, cold, detached and I never cried. I could not accept what I was seeing with my own two eyes and defiantly stuck to the only theory that gave me any feeling of control and hope. Even when my dad would say, 'Dell, why do you never ask your mother how she is? Why do you never hold her hand or brush her hair?', I would matter-of-factly tell him, 'If we act like she's sick, she'll think that she is sick.' None of this behaviour seemed bizarre or out of character to me whatsoever – in my mind, it made total sense. I was helping; I was doing the best thing for her.

In hindsight, I was, of course, utterly incapable of dealing with the emotions that accompanied my mam's potential death. I convinced myself that I was protecting her when, in fact, I was living in a fabricated reality I'd conjured up to protect me. My whole life I had felt like I was on the verge of losing her, but I couldn't lose her – I needed her more than anyone. She is my best friend, my only source of unwavering, unconditional love, support and guidance. My favourite assembly of stardust walking this earth. I have always been acutely aware that it is my greatest privilege simply to have been born of her DNA. I have never fought with her for more than a few exasperated sentences because you could never fight with her: she is compassion personified. The Einstein of emotional intelligence. Over the years, through every illness, I don't remember her complaining once. She would often tell me she'd rather it be her than any of us. I think it is this mantra that gave her the extraordinary resolute strength and grace she displayed in the face of every challenge, year after year.

In times of sickness and in those rare seasons of health, she was the architect of all the love and magic in our home when I was growing up. Her ability to make you feel like the most special person in the world with the simplest of acts is unparalleled. I treasured the days I came home from school to the smell of her stew bubbling in the kitchen and the sweet melancholy sound of her singing Sarah McLachlan's 'Angel'. I would go upstairs to drop my bag and find fresh pyjamas and slippers, warm from the heater, waiting folded on my bed alongside the newest copy of my favourite teen magazine or a face mask or a chocolate bar. Some days she would let me go into class a little late so we could take the quiet corner in the café across the road from my school gate to have a bowl of soup and a chat. She'd organise movie nights for my brother and me, an ocean of blankets and pillows in front of the blazing fire and far too much butter and salt on our popcorn, because that was how we liked it. Sometimes she would call me from the landing at the top of the stairs, and I'd go up to find she'd run me a bubble bath complete with glimmering tea lights and a glass of water with cucumber and lemon sitting on a doily on the toilet seat – a proper spa experience, she'd say. Every holiday, every birthday and every occasion was celebrated with so much thought and heart. Christmas and Halloween have always been her favourite excuses for excess, the house transformed to rival a movie set.

It is this catalogue of treasured memories triumphing over the many, many traumatic ones that are a testament to her always doing everything in her power to raise us buffered from her pain and suffering. She is the most admirable person I've encountered in my life and so it's probably unsurprising that it was her gentle, kind words that finally broke the dam of my unconscious emotional suppression.

When she wasn't being subjected to aggressive bouts of chemotherapy and radiotherapy, more holistic types of healing were encouraged as part of her treatment, things like juicing, massage, creative hobbies, yoga or journaling. My mam had never really been of the spiritual self-care persuasion, but she took to juicing like a religion and began making cards and taking pottery classes. I attended the latter with her weekly, after which we'd always frequent the same chipper. Her taste-buds were damaged from chemo so I'd have to hide the grimace and plaster on the grin after every chip, poisoned with a bounty of salt and vinegar that just about registered on her palate. She never told me she had started journaling during her treatment, but I found her small diary sitting on her bedside table at home one evening.

Still in my trance-like, numb emotional state I began to flippantly read extracts from it. There was a page or two lamenting the loss of her hair, eyebrows and eyelashes, which she felt robbed her of her femininity, advertised her illness and made her subject to streams of unwelcome stares and nods of sympathy. The alternative, a synthetic wig, only amplified the hot flushes caused by her chemically induced menopause. She refused to wear it, refused to make herself any more uncomfortable just to avoid unsettling the general public with her perfectly lovely bald head. She settled on a selection of patterned bandanas that she would sometimes accessorise with dangly earrings and always matched her outfit on a given day. She looked beautiful with her head shaved, I thought as I flipped through the pages of her deeply personal musings. I stopped on a paragraph that caught my eye because the scribble of my name popped out among the sea of slightly illegible reflections. I don't remember her words exactly, but it was something along the lines of how very, very proud she was of me for the strength, composure and maturity I was showing in the face of her diagnosis. How much she loved me and felt appreciative of the example I was setting for my young, sensitive brother who couldn't but wear his whole heart on his sleeve. I couldn't read another word, distracted by the formidable rising of a tsunami of muzzled emotion that had been concealed for over a year.

For the first time since I'd heard the word *cancer*, I sobbed until my eyes stung, burning red, and my chest ached from heaving. It started as a wail, built to a scream and finished with me an exhausted, blubbering infant curled up on her bedroom floor. It was like all of a sudden the lights went on and I was myself again – soft and scared and incredibly ashamed of how I had handled this. I felt so relieved to return to the plane of emotion yet simultaneously distressed at trying to accept what I had stubbornly labelled as rational behaviour for so long. I was overcome with the urge to hug my mam, to tell her how sorry I was and how utterly wrong but predictably compassionate it was of her to perceive my actions as strong and composed instead of entirely neurotic. I wanted to tell her I was the most scared I'd ever been in my life, let her tell me in return that it was all going to be OK and then hide under her wing until it was all over. But I couldn't let her down – I now had to be truly strong for her – and so I did apologise, profusely and for a long time after she asked me to please stop beating myself up over nothing. But I never let her know outright that I was scared she was dying – instead, I talked to her about the things we'd do when she was better and debated with her whether her hair would grow back curly.

It didn't. It grew back exactly as it had been and she slowly returned to vitality too. Cancer took a lot from my mother far too young – it left her with lymphedema in one arm, which continues to result in recurring infection and fever, and early onset osteoporosis in her bones that hinders her mobility and comfort – but it didn't take her and for that we are all eternally grateful.

∘ ∘ ∘

It's probably unsurprising that I had a very nervous disposition as a child, although this is something I've only come to recognise myself as an adult. It wasn't outwardly obvious – I loved to perform and was very outgoing. I was often cast as the lead in my drama-school plays and put in the front row of my dance-class productions. It was

an internal state of steady stress and worry that I was far too young to observe or know how to communicate, and so it would present as different minor physical symptoms that would require a GP visit every now and again. Before the age of 10 I was having colonics for awful, constant digestive problems. I would make a substantial bet that you would have struggled to find another 12-year-old more convinced of their own impending heart attack than me – to remedy this recurring notion, I would breathe into a brown paper bag. I was a textbook hypochondriac, waiting resignedly and patiently for the inevitable brain tumour. This doomsday narrative ticked away at all times beneath the surface and became my normal state of being. Neither I nor anybody close to me ever tried to make heads or tails of it. Every incident was treated in isolation and no dots were ever joined, even when I ran screaming out of my house in the middle of the night convinced I was dying, leaving my poor teenage babysitter to catch me and then attempt to calm me down, the trusty brown bag making one of its regular appearances in the aftermath. I now realise this was probably my first panic attack. I was very young and, despite how distinctly it remains in my memory, I can't recall what may have triggered it or if the bizarre episode was ever relayed to my parents on their return home. Most likely not – rural Ireland in the 1990s wasn't exactly awash with discussions about stress, mental health or their many confusing manifestations. You took a spoon of Calpol, had some flat lemonade with a slice of toast and all was right in the world.

When I was about 11 years old, I was doing an assisted pancake stretch to warm up for my dance class. My friend had the soles of her outstretched feet pressed against the inside of my outstretched ankles. She was leaning back, holding my wrists and helping to pull my chest towards the floor while pushing my legs out into what would perhaps one day become the middle splits. Neither of us had any idea how to do this rather advanced gymnastics posture effectively or safely, of course – we would just pull the other as hard as possible for as long as possible, bouncing about to alleviate any discomfort. On this occasion, mid-stretch, something popped and tore away from the inside of my right thigh, my leg recoiled involuntarily and a sharp, persistent pain moved into the space between my groin and my kneecap. I couldn't walk for weeks, but I never got any treatment to rectify whatever damage I had done – it just gradually repaired itself however it pleased. Nineteen years later, I have only just started the process of working out the scar tissue that built in that muscle and correcting the physical imbalances it created from my right hip down to my right ankle after healing without help. When I first began this mending, simply trying to sit with a straight back and my legs spread out before me in a shallow V shape was enough to elicit a pain as acute as the day the injury occurred, my muscle yelling the protective warning cry of a memory stored deep in its fibres. After months and months of steady, consistent, patient work that involves persevering through the kind of pain and discomfort that causes my body to shake and sweat, that muscle is slowly beginning to relax and rewire. Millimetre by millimetre, day by day. If I fall out of consistency, failing to work on that muscle for even just a few consecutive days, it can feel like all my progress has been lost and I'm back to square one when I try to start it up again. Anyone who's ever had an unfortunate or untreated physical injury can probably relate to this process.

I now understand that our minds store our impactful emotional memories no differently than our bodies store the physical ones. Left to tend to themselves, they become deeply ingrained like the scar tissue in my muscle, resulting in the same imbalances in our brain as in our bones. They are as easily triggered throughout a lifetime, serving as potent reminders for our survival and wellbeing. And the process of altering those neurological circuits and reversing the intensity of their associated warnings can sometimes be no less laboured.

Dell

August 19th 1988 first born, joy uncontained,
pink in the palm of my hand,
early, unexpected then, to take her place
arranged.
Wicker basket readied, soft, warm, lined with
thought and affection,
takes residence in rooms of ritual, no other had
frequented.
A thousand photos taken, store memories of
hope,
all our deepest hungers accomplished as parental
dotes.
New aromas fill the air; fresh resonances are
heeded,
primacies changed forever, anxiousness preceded.
Wakeful nights, vigilant, amateur and sombre
waits the light that ushers newer consolation.
Drawn on past comparisons that have no
relevance,
all is different now, no need for doubts or tears.
Elegance and beauty in the eyes of pater
Nonentity can deter not even natal tartar.

Wondrous, miraculous, amazing, full of
 life's hope,
nothing has compared before and nothing
 will erode.
Growing stronger, bigger and more beautiful,
 a Mary Poppins groupie.
Following her mother's steps in every domestic
 duty.
Reams and reams of drawing, pictures and
 expressions,
more to show future artistic impressions.
What incredible accomplishments so young
 and so determined,
the world of beauty, fashion and light
 entertainment.
What will tomorrow bring, who knows, who
 can determine,
all is certain is, that we will welcome its creation.

By Anthony Moyles, my dad,
written 24 *April* 2015

CHAPTER 2

my dad

'When you are in the middle of a story, it isn't a story at all, but only a confusion, a dark roaring blindness, a wreckage of shattered glass and splintered wood or else a boat crushed by the icebergs or swept over the rapids and all onboard powerless to stop it. It's only afterwards that it becomes anything like a story at all. When you are telling it to yourself or to someone else'

MARGARET ATWOOD

So often while writing this book, at the end of a day I would read back over my words to find I had settled on the funniest, easiest or most likeable version of the truth. I'm not immune to that natural impulse to be agreeable, putting my best foot forward so that you'll like me. It has been a confronting lesson in authenticity, challenging myself to rewrite those parts as they truly occurred from my perspective, no matter how that will look to others. I pushed myself to do this for two reasons: one, lying to yourself and everyone else is probably not a good thing; and two, I really believe it is only the absolute imperfect truth that will make this book a worthy pursuit and (hopefully) a relatable read. We live in a world that mostly showcases and celebrates our good days, our perfect relationships and our unattainable curated realities. In direct opposition to this insidious epidemic, I wanted to tell you my messy story with all its shadows, shortcomings and blind spots because examining these parts of myself is what ultimately led me to really understand and accept who I am, and this seemingly small feat changed everything for me. Still, even with that purpose in mind, I have rarely experienced resistance quite as distinct or unyielding as I did when it came to sitting down to write this chapter. It took me a long time and many, many rewrites because I love my dad and I never, ever want to hurt him.

I am incredibly proud to be his daughter. I admire him very much for the journey he has undertaken to become the man he is now. In our little hometown he is an eager community volunteer, a keen horticulturist, a poet and a chef, a gentle, creative soul. (By the way, for those wondering, myself included before he clarified it for me, 'natal tartar' is his poetic licence for 'birthmark'. I was born with a large one on my face, which was nicknamed 'the strawberry' until it disappeared when I was three or four.) My dad was never afforded the opportunity to explore his natural academic abilities, so he returned to university in his late forties to complete his bachelor's and master's degrees through disciplined distance learning. Now he works every day to reintroduce early school leavers who have struggled with hurdles like addiction to the education system. When we chat these days, the conversation is generally philosophical in nature – he loves to ruminate on ideas like Maslow's self-actualisation or Brian Cox's latest argument regarding the single/multiverse theory. My dad is a wise and brilliant man, arguably the most formative person in my life thus far, so it would be a sizeable side step to forgo the fact that this hasn't always been the case.

As I've mentioned already, I rarely saw my dad for a lot of my childhood and I simply didn't form much of a close relationship with him, good or bad. He worked very long and hard hours, sacrificing that precious time to provide for us as best he could. This is something I know he regrets now, but I'm sure at the time it felt like his rightful role and duty to his growing family. I was almost a teenager when he changed jobs and started to be around the house more often. It was probably our first unfortunate obstacle that we only began to get to know each other as I was moving into those awful, awkward years filled with soap-opera levels of angst, confusion and self-centredness. Add to that the fact that my dad had spent almost every day from the age of 13 up until that point, three decades later, climbing the ranks from kitchen porter to head chef. You only need to have watched one episode of any TV show featuring Gordon Ramsay to loosely understand the coping mechanisms and typical behaviours that might instil in a person.

With his blessing, I'd like to tell you our story and how it, unbeknown to me until recent years, contributed to my own glaring failings later in life.

° ° °

17 May 2004

Dear Diary,

Right, I'm going to tell you all of what just happened. Earlier today Richard was in the sitting room calling me a bitch so I gave him a harmless shove and he fell over the coffee table, knocking the bowl of marbles all over the place, and of course started roaring over nothing. I tried to explain to Dad that he was calling me a bitch and that I only gave him a little shove to shut him up, but he made me go to my room. I stayed there for about two hours and then went downstairs to get something to eat. I took a yogurt from the fridge and four Jaffa Cakes from the biscuit tin in the press and he went MAD at me! He started roaring at me to put some of them back and I said to him, 'Why? They're only biscuits!'

Well, he jumped up from the chair (you know his usual scary way) and dragged me back to the press. He slapped me across the face twice and spit all over me while he was screaming in my face. Over Jaffa Cakes! I even feel guilty for writing this, like I'm feeling sorry for myself, but I don't know what to do. Like, is he allowed to do that? Was I doing something wrong? I have to do something about this. I've tried talking to him. I don't know what to do.

Daniella x

∘ ∘ ∘

I was 15 when I wrote this. Reading it now, I can almost disassociate from the memory of how it felt and find the humour in my brazen misbehaviour and the unnecessary dramatics. But at the time my mam was battling cancer and I was quite scared of my dad, our potential single parent. I had also just learned that I would not be allowed into fourth year of secondary school because of my increasingly disruptive behaviour and even lousier results. This meant I was one of just a handful of students who would be fast-tracked to fifth year, which in my mind also meant I was about to lose all my friends. I don't know if you've ever met a teenager, but this is truly the most crippling news one could ever receive. To make matters worse, my Junior Cert exam was starting in a matter of weeks. This series of papers is usually the first time in our young lives in Ireland where our level of discipline and responsibility is measured by the state. I was extremely worried about this, on top of everything else, because I had seriously neglected to do the necessary regurgitation practice required to pass. Instead, I had been predominantly interested in mitching off class, trying to smoke rolled-up pages torn from my copybooks and sneaking out of the house via the conservatory roof in the middle of the night. No amount of stressors could deter me from being a textbook unruly teenager: it's a hard-wired, selfish rite of passage, it seems.

The night before my first exam, English Paper 1, my dad, most likely enraged by one of the above behaviours, threw a remote control halfway across the sitting room and into my face, leaving me with a throbbing headache. The following morning he yelled at me for the whole car journey from our front door to my school gates. I remember feeling the lump in my throat build to a searing pressure in my head, but I reminded myself that, no matter what, this time I would endure his tyranny in silence. I would force away the tears and I would gain another of my own small victories with stoicism. His final encouraging words, 'get the fuck out of my car', rang in my ears as I slammed his passenger door, turned on my heel and felt the warm blood stream over my lips as he pulled away. The sight of the blood was enough to shock me out of whatever state of fury I was in and the practical process of tending to the problem provided further distraction, after which I returned to a more manageable level of rage. I would get unexplained strong nosebleeds now and then throughout my teenage years – I didn't understand why at the time – but on this day the nosebleed wasn't enough of a release for my wound-up body. Midway through my first exam paper, sitting in the centre of the exam hall, perfectly silent except for the loud ticking second hand of the enormous mounted clock, the footsteps of the supervisors pacing the long aisles between tables and the frenzied scribbles of 60 or more students, I self-consciously suppressed a natural impulse to call out when half of one of my back molars crumbled out of my mouth and into my shaking hand. I must have been grinding my teeth harder than usual.

My dad and I fought like this with varying degrees of severity for the entirety of my teenage years and into early adulthood, the intensity of the hostility between us only waning due to physical distance after I moved out. When I was growing up he was generally belligerent and overbearing in how he handled me. I was constantly frustrated by my total dependence on him, on the roof he put over my head and the food he put on the table for me every day. I wanted to tell him to go fuck himself and never have to see him again, but I knew that wasn't feasible, which frustrated me further. I was resigned to the fact that we would have no relationship whatsoever after the day I turned 18 and, truthfully, I couldn't wait for that to become a reality, as awful as it is to admit.

In the meantime, there were days where we would scream at each other for hours. But I never won our fights, I never felt remotely heard and I was certainly never near the ball-park of being right about anything, so I learned to simply keep quiet and out of the way. For the guts of a decade, when he entered a room I would leave and vice versa. We avoided each other at all costs, barely uttering a word between the sporadic clashes that would erupt with the pressurised expulsion of a volcano – or, in my case, the capillaries in my nose. I thought he was arrogant, rude and cruel. He thought I was a disrespectful, ungrateful brat. I resented him so much for the eggshell atmosphere he created in our house, one I felt he relished. But of course, he didn't. He, too, hated every minute of the painful, complicated exchanges that became our norm. But at the time, neither he nor I had enough life experience, self-awareness or education to even begin to make sense of our erratic emotions and damaging behaviours. We were equally hot-headed and stubborn. Something else we shared was a strong sense of guilt over the ripple effects our relationship had on the rest of our family and the home that they had to live in too. It was a very uncomfortable daily existence for us all, and I reduced the blame for this down to him alone and he did the same to me. What could have been a common ground and a reasonable basis for negotiations simply perpetuated the anger between us again, a hamster wheel of contempt.

Ironically, or perhaps obviously to the empaths and trained therapists reading, despite the contradiction of our apparent behaviours described so far, my dad and I are both extremely sensitive people. He never got to be a teenager, too burdened by employment from a young age, but he did learn early on that he lived in a world that rewarded alpha males: parading noxious levels of masculinity and emotional unavailability was praised, while the slightest expression of feeling or sensitivity was ridiculed. This social standard couldn't have been more antagonistic to his tender nature, and I believe he built a suit of armour and suppressed that side of himself to get by. My dad resided almost entirely in a protective, one-dimensional version of his much broader, brilliant self for decades, until I think he nearly forgot the other parts of him existed.

To pare this back to the most simplistic explanation, not feeling free or able to be yourself is really not good for you. It's exhausting, reductive and causes significant mental discomfort, to put it lightly. But it was all he knew for a very long time and I think it produced a lot of pain and anger in him, which, alongside his environmental conditioning, emerged as some pretty shitty, maladjusted conduct with regards to me. And that's worth pointing out: this was the reality of our relationship alone – my mother and brother met this side of him on occasion, but for the most part seemed to know a different man than I did. For a long time I couldn't understand this – I felt singled out and bullied. But now, as a partially functioning adult, I have come to recognise that, outside of those environmental dissimilarities that shaped us individually, my dad and I are undeniably cut from the same cloth. For a start, I am his mini-me in terms of appearance, but more than that, we are mirrored in our natural tendencies, reflexive reactions and nuances of personality to the point that we drive each other mental. We are a gift to each other in that we highlight each other's weakest parts with our alikeness. As is often the case, the people who bother or provoke us the most do so because we see in them the things we don't like in ourselves.

For most of my life I rarely gave any thought or significance to my dysfunctional relationship with my dad growing up or to the effects it may or may not have had on me. It was just another commonplace story and I was happy to put it behind me – 'daddy issues' is a common phrase for a reason – but I was never going to be able to leave it behind if I wanted to pursue real happiness. I didn't know it then, but my dad had handed me down his suit of armour and his survival-based hyper-masculinity. He unintentionally taught me some destructive patterns of behaviour, detrimentally weak boundaries and adverse means of coping with conflict and stress. He was the only influential male figure in my life, and as I grew older I continued to struggle to form healthy relationships with men. Every unsuspecting guy who entered my life in any significant way, with even the best of intentions, was met with the same passive-aggressive reactivity and overarching pessimism, unfavourably paired with that strange approval-seeking behaviour I had acted out in my relationship with my dad. I was just too young to understand that you have to heal what's hurt you or you'll bleed on people who didn't cut you.

In lots of ways I moved through the world like a wrecking ball and took no responsibility for it, hurting others and myself with my own pain and ignorance. Often a whisper from my gut told me there was something wrong with some of the ways I acted, but I didn't know how to fix it or more likely didn't want to face up to the task. There were beneficial traits, of course, one being a fiercely independent streak in every possible way from the day I was old enough to leave home. I preferred to focus on those. But ultimately the bad outweighed the good and I was forced to take a long, hard look at myself and why I was the way I was. In his mid-fifties, life forced my dad on a similar journey, one that brought us back together and allowed us to mend our relationship. This is a cruel cliffhanger, but the resolution to our story and how it occurred will unfold throughout the pages of this book – we're just not quite there yet.

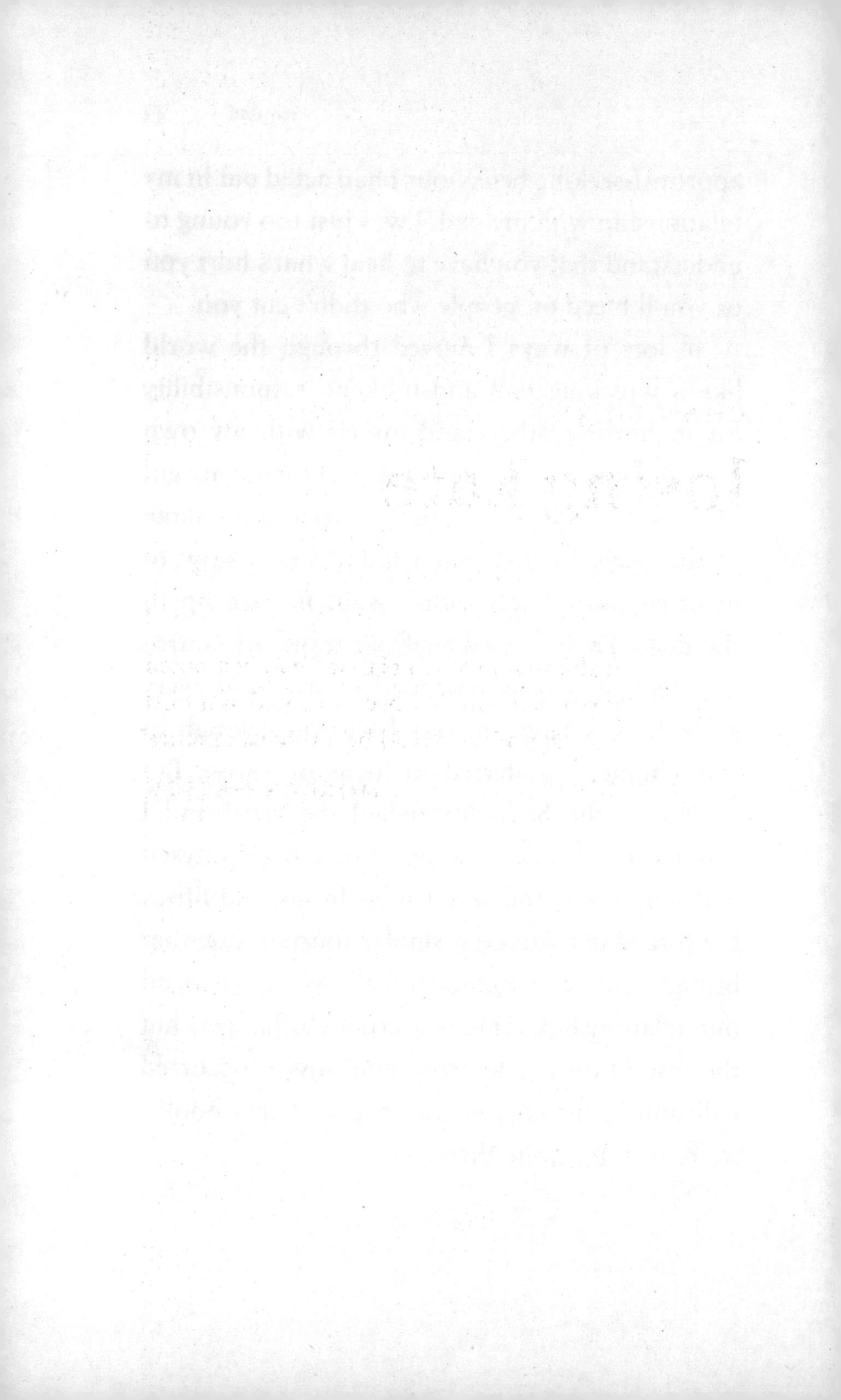

CHAPTER 3

losing kate

'A thousand moments that I had just taken
for granted – mostly because I had assumed
that there would be a thousand more'

MORGAN MATSON

One of the greatest gifts of my teenage years was the considerable lifelong blessing of my group of girlfriends.

Earlier, I mentioned that devastating moment when, aged 15, I was told I wouldn't be allowed into fourth year of secondary school – presumably because my tortured year head and principal wanted me out of there and off their list of annoyances ASAP! And please, let me clarify: I was annoying. It was with good reason the powers that be in my school didn't let me into transition year, which, in essence, is a year off the normal curriculum – they knew I'd take extravagant advantage of that, so much so that I might be entirely unable to re-enter normal schooling with its rigid regulations to complete my basic education. Whoever made the call did me an enormous favour, but at the time it felt like nothing short of a catastrophe. A lot of the girls I'd been in school with since the age of four or five were no longer going to be part of my day to day. I would have to acquaint myself with the 'older girls', girls who'd had well-established cliques of their own since they, too, were four or five.

I was intimidated and panicked at the thought of the summer holidays ending; a school I'd grown to know my place in so well was about to become unfamiliar again. There were just 10 or so of us moving up from my school year to be mixed with the students from the year above us. I knew we'd be split evenly among five base classes that were to be formed, with roughly 30 students in each. Now, I was never great at maths, but by my calculations that meant I would know one, perhaps two, girls in my class. The rest would be almost strangers, faces that had passed me in a hallway.

By the time the new school year commenced, I had created so much fear in my mind and played through so many negative scenarios that

I inevitably struggled for the first few months. Granted, it was a daunting transition at an age where your social circle and their opinion of you is your prevailing concern in life. To get by, I practised my favourite coping mechanism: complete avoidance. I skipped class or pretended to be sick to stay home, and when I did make it to school, I generally kept to myself. But with the passing of time came the necessity to admit defeat, to finally accept this awful fate that had been forced upon me, and once I stopped arguing with reality, some frankly life-changing things happened.

I realised that lots of the girls, not just in my base class but also my curriculum classes throughout the day, were nice. Like, really nice. I saw that they were warm, genuine, chatty, funny, kind, generous, helpful and all-round wonderful, once my presumptuous brain stopped perpetuating the notion that they would be otherwise. It was a self-fulfilling prophecy: I had made a false prediction about the new girls I would be interacting with, which had evoked in me a way of behaving towards them, which in turn made my false prediction come true. It was my first experience of a life lesson that would manifest many times before I fully registered it: your attitude matters and your mindset undoubtedly shapes your experiences.

It's now 16 years later and Michelle is still one of my best friends. I distinctly remember that she was the one who first extended an olive branch of friendship to mix with her gang of girls, who had mostly known each other since playschool. I also remember being nervous on the initial occasions that we hung out or chose to sit together in class because I thought they were all very cool. They had boyfriends and they went to parties with the equally cool older guys from the all-boys school across town. At the time I didn't think I could stack up or fit in. But that simple gesture started a domino effect that not only drastically improved my teenage years, but has also resulted in one of the greatest privileges of my adult life: my place in a rare and glorious group of 16 girls who have been each other's supporters, confidants and mentors for nearly two decades. Their names are Laura, Niamh, Áine, Amy, Ciara, Fiona, Jill, another Laura, Lynn, Orlaith, Ruth, Steph, Tara, Tracy and, of course, Michelle. Now the art of storytelling requires that I build an incrementally revealing and relatable character profile for each of my friends named above, one that gives them depth and heart and makes you wish they were your friend too. But that could fill an entire series of novels, so you'll just have to take my word for it that they are all individually phenomenal people that I wholeheartedly admire and thank my lucky stars for every day. It's something we discuss openly and regularly – how lucky we are to have found each other and stuck together like we have all these years. We've been part of all the biggest milestones of each other's lives so far – every first love, eighteenth, twenty-first and thirtieth, every graduation, promotion, first home, engagement, marriage and baby shower. And I can promise you, if any one of us ever tried to pull some nonsense like a gender-reveal party, we would be swiftly reminded of where we came from and stripped of such notions. They are the salt of the earth, and over the years we've helped to carry each other through heartbreak, loss and injury, through all of life's inescapable stress and pressure. Individually and as a collective, we have always celebrated each other's successes and done our best to buffer each other's failures. We genuinely root for one another, and that is a rare gift to find in such a big group.

I don't know who or where I would be without these girls and I don't know why I got the golden ticket to bypass the stereotypical teenage-girl dramas that can sometimes roll on for a lifetime. They have always naturally placed a solid emphasis on the positive, on gratitude, on being uplifting rather than judgemental. Disagreements happened over the years, of course, but they've always been resolved without biases forming or melodramas dragging them out. And I am so damn grateful that this has been the foundation of my understanding of female relationships, that these are the expectations and behaviours I have carried with me out into the world. It made me a girl's girl from the get-go, mostly naive to competition, bitching or scrambles for hierarchy, and considering my previously noted dysfunctional tendencies with men, it's a relief that I could interact reasonably with at least one gender. It is thanks to these girls that I fell somewhat in love with my last two years of school – and that I soon required the regular use of my cousin Kate's ID to get into the local nightclub that I was a couple of years too young to frequent.

Kate was six years older than me and she was my favourite cousin. That actually means something because I have a large pool of extended family to choose from, roughly 56 cousins in total when you combine all the children from both sides. I looked up to Kate in a way I never fully understood until I didn't have her there to look up to any more. I got my hair done with her hairdresser and my nails done in her preferred salon. When she got a small cluster of simple stars tattooed on her left bum cheek, I followed suit soon after with a string of nautical stars tattooed on mine. That choice wasn't driven by a particular affiliation with the ocean or a nod to my seafaring days – I just thought they looked cool. I've since realised I may have been mistaken, but I love them now, regardless, as a permanent reminder of her. When I was still very young, I would ask to have sleepovers at her house, which was on the isolated edge of the Curragh in Kildare. On one such occasion, we snuck out into the darkness of a late evening in winter, her in her early teens and me still a minor, navigating fields and traversing motorway bridges on an adventure to the nearest VCR rental store, Xtravision, a good 30-minute jaunt away. Stocked up on movies and junk food, the excitement of a night of pure escapism and indulgence beckoning, we arrived home to a furious greeting from both sets of our parents. They had been tipped off by a concerned passer-by who had recognised us crossing that motorway bridge, two unaccompanied kids drunk on freedom in the dark of night. Our sleepover was abruptly cancelled and I was devastated, wailing the whole way home in the car, bemoaning the end of an adventure that felt like it was only beginning.

Towards the end of my teenage years, Kate and I bonded over more than our rebellious tendencies or a penchant for acrylics and misguided body markings. She understood my tumultuous relationship with my dad and hated her big 'Moyles nose' with the same passion as I hated mine. We would sometimes discuss how a nose job was the only option for us if we were ever to become gorgeous, successful models. But truthfully, I never aspired to become a model with any degree of seriousness, mainly because I didn't think I was a particularly attractive person and my dreams at the time extended only to getting through the next day. I had the long, scrawny limbs, but Kate was the beautiful one – she had model credentials that eclipsed her petite five-foot-one stature. I also knew I didn't have the confidence – life overwhelmed me regularly – but not Kate. She appeared to cope with the undulating nature of existence with equal amounts of ease and vigour. She fell pregnant with her precious daughter, Ella, aged 17. Nine months later, on a Sunday in June, she gave birth in just three hours, then started her Leaving Certificate exam on the Wednesday, three days later, from the same hospital bed. Ella was her greatest gift and her proudest accomplishment, of which she had already amassed an impressive list.

She was a gifted Irish dancer. Practising from the age of four, she became a senior champion and highly regarded dance teacher, holding the title of Council Register on the dancing council committee. She and her sister Evelyn danced together, winning more awards than any other set locally, which kept the floors, shelves, windowsills and mantelpieces of the rooms in their family home decorated with gold trophies, medals and award ribbons. Kate was also a skilled pianist – her favourite piece to play was 'The Entertainer' by Scott Joplin or one of the melodies from *Miss Saigon*. Even when she was heavily pregnant, she would lean over her growing bump for hours to practise for her practical piano exams. To this day

I have never played an instrument, but accounting for my unmitigated musical inability, she taught me to perform Celine Dion's 'My Heart Will Go On' with a single hand like I was Chopin. I was so in awe of her and the talent I scored just from being around her that nearly two decades later, I can still remember every chord exactly as she showed me.

I was 17 when I finished secondary school, a year younger than the average student because of skipping fourth year. This was both a blessing and a curse. On the one hand, I was free from a system I mostly loathed a year in advance of my scheduled release date, but on the other, I was too young to enjoy the compulsory summer of partying and celebrations stress-free. Thankfully, house parties were a common occurrence and I had been working as a barmaid at the weekends for a couple of years in a popular local pub, so all the staff there knew me. They were fond of me too, the baby on the roster, and because of that I could generally get my hands on a couple of drinks without any hassle when it was the chosen spot for a night out. But when the festivities commenced or culminated at the local nightclub, I was always the uncertainty in the group. Getting past the venue's bouncers became my favourite summer pastime, an emotional rollercoaster with mixed results.

Sometimes I would breeze straight by, deep in distracted, hilarious conversation with a friend, exuding the unflappable confidence of a well-established 18-year-old ready and willing to flash their ID with an irritated undertone. When I was stopped my chance of success was 50/50, but I'd always come prepared – it was very important to be sober(ish), dressed to look the part and with my answers well rehearsed. Kate had given me her expired college ID card; it was peeling at the edges and had a tiny, grainy, mostly indistinguishable image of her in the right-hand corner. Still, it helped that we looked like sisters. It showed her full name, college course, student number and date of birth, and I could reel all of this and more off without hesitating for a nano-second. Sometimes I was turned away without explanation, other times it was because I had no secondary up-to-date ID. But on the occasions I was given that subtle cherished nod to pass, the relief would wash over me, quickly followed by uncontainable excitement for the gift of a night of memories that might have never been. The joy was always amplified when I met Kate, who had also been asked for ID, inside the club and we would cheers all night to outsmarting security.

The biggest night of that summer was our Leaving Certificate results night. I hadn't applied to, and so naturally hadn't been accepted on, any college course, so there was no particular reason for me to be extra jubilant. But I had passed with an average grade after years of reading magazines hidden between the pages of my schoolbooks during study and that was enough to justify celebrating aggressively! For the night that was in it, Kate had upgraded my fake ID to her passport, accompanied by her driver's licence for additional proof if necessary. The whole town was going to be overrun with hysterical teenagers, so she had no need for either – she wouldn't be venturing out into the frenzy.

The girls and I were getting ready in Amy's house. I'd got a fresh T-bar of highlights the day before, bought a new dress and picked up a naggin and a ten pack of Silk Cut Purple for the pre-drinks. I was one of those terrible social smokers that never actually bought a box of cigarettes, but there was a buzz in the air that evening, an eager anticipation for the craic to come, and

I wanted to be generous. At around 10.30 p.m., all of us tipsy, parading excessively shimmering tanned limbs and poker-straight hair, we began filing into taxis and demanding Rihanna be played at eardrum-bursting volume en route to the nightclub. The queue was out the door and around the corner when we arrived. I was only a week shy of turning 18 and, armed with more valid ID than I'd ever had, my confidence was at an all-time high – so high that, for once, the usual planning to make sure I got past security hadn't even come up in conversation with the girls.

For 30 minutes we snaked closer and closer to the familiar muddy-cocktailed aroma of smoke, sweat and sick wafting from the double-door entrance. We barely noticed the persistent covering of goose bumps on our overly exposed skin, kept warm by a steady stream of laughter and concealed shots from the caps of our vodka bottles. Almost at the head of the queue, I could feel the bass vibrate beneath my feet. I made eye contact with the lady manning the cloakroom just inside the door and she smiled at me – surely a sign that this was a sure thing. The girls streamed in ahead of me, uninterrupted except for a single swift bag check. Following close behind, riding their coattails to a night of too many tequilas, my bold stride was suddenly obstructed by the arm of a young bouncer I didn't recognise. 'ID please, miss.'

I was rattled but still in the game. 'No problem,' I replied as nonchalantly as possible as the last of the girls slipped by, side-eyes ablaze with concern.

'I know Kate Moyles – you're not Kate Moyles,' he said on presentation of my driver's licence.

'Yes, I am,' I persisted. 'Maybe you know another Kate Moyles?'

I waved my passport at him. He examined it closely, looked up at me blankly and said, 'No, miss. I know this Kate Moyles, right here in these pictures, and it's certainly not you. Now, I'll be keeping both of these IDs and you can step out of the queue.'

There was no reasonable argument I could make. Standing on the other side of the cheap red velvet rope, my phone lighting up with texts from the girls and my eyes filling with tears, I called Kate.

Suddenly it was freezing. A few minutes later, sitting on the cold pavement with my carefully applied mascara streaming down my heavily made-up cheeks, just a stone's throw from the good times unfolding inside, I saw Kate hastily turn the corner in her tiny rattling bottle-green Volkswagen Polo. She hopped out, slammed the door and paced past me, arms swinging and chest puffed. Her tiny frame presented no obstacle to her giving the bouncer who had stopped me a slap on the back of his large head. He turned, started to laugh and attempted to calm her down but she was unstoppable, yelling at him for being a 'life-ruining dickhead who needs to take his head out of his arse', among other things. She tried her best to fight my corner, but the decision was made and none of the door staff was going to budge, especially when her impassioned performance played out in front of the dwindling queue – they had to make their point. Exasperated, she snatched her ID from the young bouncer's hand, gave him one last playful thump on the arm for good measure and came to sit beside me on the kerb. 'We'll celebrate tonight together, Dell. I never got to properly mark my Leaving Cert either because I preferred to stay home with Ella, so this one is for both of us.'

o o o

Seven months later, Kate died in a car accident. She was 24.

She had just dropped Ella, who was five at the time, to school and was driving to her job at the medical centre in the small, quaint village of Sallins in County Kildare. It was a very foggy morning and, unbeknown to her, there had already been a 60-car pile-up over a 5 kilometre stretch of the motorway she took every day on her route to work. Hers was one of the last cars to make it onto the road before authorities closed it. She hit the back of a fire engine parked at the scene of the first number of collisions, and even though the engine's blue lights and sirens were in use, there were no skid marks at the scene – visibility was so poor that she didn't even brake before impact. Twenty-nine people were hospitalised after the accident that morning, but there was only one fatality: our beautiful, brilliant Kate.

She'd suffered serious injuries to her head and chest. She was slight but she was mighty, and she fought for nearly 24 hours after the crash, until every person who loved her and her vibrant, magnetic personality had had the chance to say goodbye. In the early hours of the following morning, with the people closest to her by her bedside, Kate took her last breath and, just like that, her irreplaceable light was gone.

Kate's death shocked me to my core. It cracked open the foundation of everything I thought I knew about the world at the time. I was 18, so I had lost grandparents and relatives to old age or illness. I had experienced my own mother's far too frequent dance with mortality too. I knew death loomed near and inevitable, but never in my young life had I learned so explicitly how fleeting, precious and unpredictable our existence could be. There was nowhere to hide from the all-consuming pain and grief of losing Kate. There was no respite, no relief.

I remember one particularly vivid moment from the hazy, idle hours after she passed. My extended family had decided to congregate at a hotel near the hospital for sandwiches and tea, a gathering to cushion each other's dismay yet remain close enough to Kate, ready to mobilise on a second's notice for any reason necessary. We pulled into the car park and I asked for a few minutes alone in the car. The short drive from the hospital to the hotel had broken my heart. Everywhere I looked after leaving the bubble of the ICU, people were getting on with their lives – laughing, chatting, shopping, eating and jogging. Did they not realise what had just happened? I wanted the world to stop turning on account of this loss. It felt only right that everyone should be in mourning with us. I was paralysed by the cruel realisation of death's permanency and, in stark contrast, life's unremitting onward momentum. Something so obvious to me now was absolutely life-altering to me then. Much to the concern of my parents, over an hour passed in the blink of an eye while I ruminated in the back seat of the car, assimilating a tragic new understanding of the world between making direct calls to Kate's voicemail to hear her sweet voice. I thought she was gone forever, disappeared into the abyss, and while that is fact in a physical sense, in truth Kate has never left me. Even in the brief bouts of sleep I managed to find over the months following her death, I would see her in my dreams. And to this day, well over a decade later, the ripple of her effect on my life is still very clear.

Until Kate's death I was adrift, uninspired and generally quite angry at the world. Losing her elevated me out of this mindset with force. I felt fearless, emboldened by the sudden acute awareness of my own momentary existence. Death has a way of clearing away everything that doesn't matter, and what I saw now was that we all think we have time. We all think we will have the privilege of repeating our happy moments, of seeing the people we love the most again tomorrow, of growing old, when all we truly have is the privilege of right now. I understood with clarity that I, and no one else, would be the engineer of my own adventure and I was ravenous to take on every precious day she'd never get to see.

A secondary, less life-altering conclusion I also came to was that I would never get that nose job we'd planned together in detail. It was a feature we shared and I would keep it, proud, prominent and imperfect, just the way it was.

CHAPTER 4

the lovely girls competition

'Making a decision is only the beginning of things. When someone makes a decision, he is really diving into a strong current that will carry him to places he had never dreamed of when he first made the decision'

PAULO COELHO

I've always craved independence and instinctively prioritised my freedom, generally resisting the incremental responsibilities of life that we tend to amass as we age. After finishing school, during that summer, autumn and winter before the season of Kate's passing, I worked two jobs to facilitate the former. The smoking ban had been introduced in Ireland, and with it my long shifts in the pub became less sickening, my lungs no longer lined with the second-hand tar of a hundred patrons by clock-out. But my mam had handed me down her crumbling, embarrassingly noisy maroon Ford Fiesta after I passed my driving test (first attempt, in case you're interested) and

I was eager to explore new career options in new pastures.

I ventured 20 minutes up the road to the neighbouring town of Newbridge, where I worked as a sales assistant in a Meteor store during the day. I enjoyed the motivation of having monthly targets and honed my spiel to coax every person who walked in to sign a bill-pay contract, for the benefit of my commission. In the evenings I waitressed at a local restaurant, a posh establishment by my standards. I always felt a little out of place dressed in my crisp white work shirt, attempting to bluff my way through a recommendation for one of our many bottles of expensive red wine. In hindsight, my discomfort probably came down to the fact that I was a terrible waitress. I always filled the wineglasses far too high, which irritated the management but resulted in great tips. I once ordered five prime fillet steaks instead of five chicken breasts by pressing the wrong tab on the electronic ordering system linking us to the kitchen staff. And then there was that occasion I was sent home …

Fancy restaurants always use so many unnecessary plates. Soup, for instance, is served in a bowl. But that bowl will then be placed on a rustic slate, which sits just inside another larger bowl with a specially made hollow for a miniature burning ember or something like that. And I get it, it's an art. But honestly, it's most inconsiderate to the waitstaff. During peak hours, the more experienced of us would carry four servings on two arms. That's a plate in each hand and another perched perilously behind on each forearm. It was a skill I just couldn't master due to the excessive plating combined with my non-existent upper body strength. But tired of double runs to the kitchen and feeling professionally impaired by my weak limbs, I decided it was time to overcome this hurdle. In preparation, I observed that dessert had the least number of decorative extras per serving: I would start there.

That evening, the family of four I was attending to, without a hitch so far, ordered four chocolate brownies and I knew this was my moment. Each brownie was served on two small plates, one slightly bigger than the other, solely for aesthetic purposes. That was just eight plates in total to balance: I could do it. A little shaky, I loaded up in the kitchen, but my confidence grew with each stride towards their table. With the last double-plating placed, I stood before them with pride, head held high and an accomplished smile and said, 'Enjoy your dessert!' Retreating to the kitchen through the open restaurant, I wondered why they had been staring at me so strangely in the aftermath of my impressive waitressing. Whatever conclusion I was about to come to was interrupted by my boss marching towards me and swiftly redirecting me behind the stone wall of the wine cellar.

'Have you got another shirt?' he barked.

Confused, I looked down at my stark white shirt to see that my boobs had both turned a deep shade of gooey brown. I had obviously instinctively used them to stabilise the brownies on my forearms. I really was a terrible waitress.

I was still living with my parents at the time, so my monthly expenditure was almost nothing. Most of my friends had left for college, taking with them our budding social life, so nights out became a rarity for me. I didn't care for shopping and I hadn't discovered any expensive habits or hobbies. Instead, I watched my earnings from the two jobs build in my student account month after month, only dipping into it for the petrol that got me to and from work in my economical hand-me-down hatchback. Life was a little beige, I suppose. I had a vague plan to rent a room in Dublin and perhaps apply to art college the following term, but as it turned out, this period of uninspired, work-focused routine soon provided the means for a Technicolor explosion of spontaneous living in the months after we lost Kate. That tragic crash happened in March of the spring after I finished secondary school, after which my approach to life got a drastic overhaul.

That April, I flew to London and bought my dream car – an almost-new black Mini Cooper One with a brown leather interior, special alloys and tinted windows. I paid for it in cash from my savings and then drove the five hours from the city to Holyhead in Wales to catch the ferry home. Don't ask me why I didn't just buy one in Ireland. The car I liked most over the course of my day or two of research must have been that one in London. I was a woman on a mission, no longer living for tomorrow when today is all we're guaranteed. I would take that famed 'life is short, buy the shoes' mentality and crank it up a few hundred notches from there on out.

Unfortunately, the car was a complete dud. Within a couple of months of finishing the mountain of paperwork it took to register it in Ireland and then tax and insure it, the power-steering pump failed, soon followed by the clutch, the automatic transmission and the timing belt in near unison. I eventually offloaded it to a garage for a sizeable loss, but I didn't care. I understood now that life was for living with all that you've got. Every bit of good is a gift and a blessing; every inevitable bump is a lesson. I couldn't play it safe any more for fear things wouldn't turn out my way – I'd already learned they were unlikely to.

In May I entered a preliminary heat for the Miss Ireland beauty pageant through the Dublin radio station Spin 103.8. They were playing a heavily produced, attention-grabbing advert on repeat, promoting their search for a Miss Ireland entry between songs from their teen-focused Hot 30 music playlist. I must have heard it a hundred times before I finally called my friend Orlaith and asked her to sit with me while I filled out the online application. She took two pictures of me on my dad's tiny Canon compact, one face-on and one profile, which I had to upload for entry alongside a long questionnaire. We worked together to populate this with appropriately strait-laced answers.

Just a few weeks before we'd lost Kate, I had cheered her on as she competed in her own heat to be crowned Miss Kildare, which would have secured her place in the same Miss Ireland pageant I was now attempting to enter. She had worn my debs dress for the occasion. I had never had much purpose or direction in my life up to this point, and even less desire to become Miss Ireland, but now I was determined to win for her. With all the county entries picked there were only a few spots left, reserved for businesses that would sponsor an entry as a marketing tool. Even with my conviction ablaze, I couldn't help feeling that a radio station like Spin 103.8 was highly unlikely to call me back. Surely my application would be lost among the sea of beautiful rich girls from Dublin's abundance of private schools.

A couple of mornings later, as I was opening the store in Newbridge, my phone rang. It was the improbable call-back and my interview with the station's management was scheduled for a day later. I couldn't concentrate for my entire work shift; I don't think I signed even one bill-pay contract. As it turned out, the interview was to narrow down the station's long list of entries to just 15 girls who would take part in the preliminary heat, a glitzy affair due to take place in Dublin's Tripod nightclub just over a week later. The event's judging panel was announced as Calum Best, Bianca Gascoigne (Paul Gascoigne's glamour-model daughter) and Michelle Heaton from Liberty X. I was in way over my head. But as soon as I pulled into my parents' driveway after getting stuck in two hours of commuter traffic on the way home from the interview, they called again to say I had secured my spot in the group of 15 finalists. I momentarily cursed Kate before panic flooded my train of thought entirely. I had no idea what I was doing and no one to ask how to do it. Despite all my drama-school training and altar-serving practice growing up, I was suddenly nauseated at the idea of parading myself in front of a room of strangers. Plus there was the small issue of the swimwear round that was to take place between the club-wear round and the on-stage interview.

The week that followed was a blur of work shifts and rushed, senseless preparations. But

Kate was with me that night as I strode with feigned poise across the confetti-littered, strobe-lit dance floor in my black bikini, my facial muscles twitching from the permanent smile. It must have been a really proud moment for my parents when, still half-dressed, I was presented with my plastic crown and winner's sash by a rowdy Calum Best in front of the unimpressed extended family members and friends of the other 14 contestants. As bizarre as this entire scene sounds – and trust me, no one thought it was more bizarre than me – this is actually the moment my aimless life found some shallow roots and my trajectory changed.

The Miss Ireland pageant took place at the end of July. I had spent the six weeks post-heat and pre-pageant juggling my two jobs with a newfound, slightly terrifying interest from the Irish media. As part of the build-up to the event, there were some promotional obligations for us contestants – photo shoots for newspapers and magazines as well as radio or television interviews. It was my introduction to a whole new world. Unsurprisingly, my story of entering on behalf of my young, beautiful cousin who had recently passed away as the result of a very public tragedy stood out, gaining particular traction. It had generated enough column inches and conversations that by the time the competition rolled around, I had been the bookie's favourite to win for a while. I still had no idea what I was doing and now, on top of that, I was overwhelmed by all the unexpected exposure. But my family was proud, Kate's family was glad for the positive preservation of her memory and it gave us all something light and uplifting to focus on at that otherwise miserable time.

To cut a long story short, I didn't win that coveted title of Miss Ireland 2007 – perhaps in part because of my unmanageable nerves, or maybe it came down to my obnoxious commitment to silver glitter and diamanté jewels. To me, these screamed pageant winner, so I clutched at them as the only certainty I had in an otherwise confusing circus. On the night of the final, I decorated myself aggressively in both like they were some kind of reflective safety blanket. My hair, my eyelids, my skin in general, my dress, my shoes and my accessories were all blindingly sparkly. 'Sure how could ya've won – they couldn't see ya through the glare off ya,' my uncle (who didn't know what a pageant was prior to this) had offered in an attempt at comfort and reassurance in the days after the competition. But I wasn't upset at having missed out on the crown because much to my disbelief, after placing third overall, I was offered a modelling contract with Assets Model Agency in Dublin. The snowballing of change in my life at this time felt rapid and uncontrollable. A few assertive decisions had blown the boundaries of my world wide open and I had somehow found myself standing at the precipice of the previously unattainable dream that Kate and I had had for ourselves.

And so it was at the beginning of August, less than six months after Kate's death, that I booked my first modelling job: a photocall for Sunway Holidays outside the St Stephen's Green Shopping Centre at the top of Grafton Street. They were promoting an end-of-summer flash sale for their package holidays to a handful of sunny southern European countries. The 'photocall' phenomenon was unique to the Irish modelling industry. When I started working it was in its infancy, but it became the daily bread-and-butter for a lot of Irish models over the years to come – in large part thanks to Georgia Salpa, a strikingly beautiful half-Greek half-Irish fellow Miss Ireland

2007 contestant turned model who soon became a household name and photocall staple.

The standard open photocall lasted for one hour, during which every tabloid and broadsheet newspaper in the country could send a dedicated photographer to capture whatever was being promoted to fill some column inches in the following day's papers. Unsurprisingly, models in bikinis always got the best coverage, sometimes even the front page! The photocall could be for a new cholesterol-lowering drug or something equally unsexy, but we'd still generally be briefed to bring a bikini. Any business could promote any product or service with a photocall by contacting a PR company, who would then hire the models for the job through our respective agencies. It was cheap and effective marketing, and the starting rate for an unknown model was around €150 to €200 for the hour. Having worked for minimum wage my whole life, pass me the bikini!

All I knew about this first job was that I had to meet the client and their PR representatives at 9 a.m. at the aforementioned location, wearing a red bikini. I didn't sleep a wink the night before, partially because I was convinced I would snooze through my 6 a.m. alarm, set so early because I anticipated needing 15 minutes to get ready, two hours to sit in traffic and at least 45 minutes to figure out how and where to park – Dublin was still an exotic and intimidating labyrinth of one-way streets to me in those days. To prepare as best I could, I had borrowed a set of my mam's various-sized rollers and entangled them into my hair with no finesse whatsoever in an attempt to create that effortless Victoria's Secret-style beachy wave. I couldn't lie down flat because of them, and my struggle to sleep sitting upright was extremely frustrating and unsuccessful. But I was a model now: beauty had to come first. That's also how I justified the noxious smell of fake tan radiating from every limb. I had applied three thick layers in the hopes it would coat my pasty skin and my growing self-doubt.

Thankfully, I managed to get there on time, find parking and produce poses I didn't know I was capable of. I assumed the role of a confident stranger, one who didn't think this whole scenario was utter lunacy, and so, standing in a bikini on a freezing cold morning in the middle of a very public thoroughfare in the city centre, my first hour as a paid professional model passed in a blur. It was humiliating, but more than that it was exhilarating.

The next day, I went to the newsagent's first thing with my mam to see that the photocall had landed in three tabloid newspapers. She bought 10 copies of each, and so began her faithful obsession with collecting every piece of material my face was printed on. My model agent at the time was called Mags and she called me that morning, asking, 'Love, did you put on any make-up?' I told her I had, when in reality all I had done was retreat beneath the safety net of my glitter addiction – one swipe across both eyelids, a quick lick of mascara, some Vaseline on my lips and I was out the door. My mam rarely wore make-up, I had no sisters to learn from and my friends and I were far from make-up artists, so how to apply it correctly was mostly a mystery to me. Still, I thought it was kind of Mags to zoom in on just that one inadequacy when she could have so easily grilled me on the unsuccessful frizzy bird's nest on my head, my menacing bloodshot eyes or the fact that I'd apparently changed ethnicity from so much fake tan.

To keep my days free for any modelling work I might be lucky enough to book, I had decided to leave my preferred job at the Meteor store (I would maintain my evening and weekend shifts in the restaurant, much to my manager's annoyance), so it being midweek and I being idle, Mags told me to come by the agency office that day for a make-up lesson from one of the more experienced models. She also said not to worry, that the photographer's flash must have washed out my make-up work and I just needed to learn how to have a heavier hand. We both knew she was being nice: it had been a bright, crisp morning; not one of the photographers had used a flash.

I had felt out of place before, but I never knew what imposter syndrome was until I walked into that agency for the first time with a sweaty upper lip from trying to parallel park. It was located in a small basement space on Lower Leeson Street and, for whatever reason, every high-profile model on their books at the time seemed to be there when I arrived. Glenda Gilson, Pippa O'Connor, Miss Ireland 2006 Sarah Morrissey and Andrea Roche, among others, filled the cramped office with busied, upbeat conversation and a level of confidence that fascinated me. They were all paralysingly beautiful, like incredibly attractive aliens. I had never been interested in fashion, but I was suddenly distinctly aware of how scruffy my 'dressy pants' were. I had usually reserved these good loose-fitting linen trousers for non-uniform days at school paired with runners – the ends would drag along the ground and had turned a permanent shade of dirt, even after washing. I did not look or feel the part and I now desired to get through this appointment quickly and quietly.

At one point during my make-up tutorial – a far more complicated and choreographed routine of brushes and products than I could have anticipated, even long before the era of contour – Andrea Roche shouted 'Daniella!' and I instinctively jumped up and yelled back '*Yes?*', only to realise she was calling after another model's young daughter of the same name who was running dangerously close to some steps. I don't think she even noticed my outburst in the hustle and bustle of the office, but I was mortified. I replayed it in my head for days afterwards, my cheeks burning at the memory, and practised the different explanations I could offer if I was to ever cross paths with her again.

In spite of everyone's best attempts to be courteous and friendly to me that day in the office,

I had barely spoken by the time I snuck out the door to leave. My churning feelings of embarrassment and inadequacy soon lifted when I noticed that my car had been clamped on the street outside, replaced by the searing certainty that I had stepped into a world I was just not cut out for.

° ° °

Over the course of the year that followed, I gradually found my feet within the industry. And I never did explain myself to Andrea Roche on any of the many times I saw her – I decided it had been a completely forgettable moment for her and instead took it as an acknowledgment of my own irrational self-consciousness. I also decided that in my case, the term 'model' and its connotations could be applied very loosely, as I said yes to every job the agency offered. Alongside weekly photocalls, I was an amateur boxing-ring girl, I would stand for days flogging leaflets at any junket and I played hostess on the door of any nightclub that would have me. I was hooked by the strange, varied and often exciting nature of the business and it was always extraordinary to me when a booking came into the agency with my name attached. It felt as though I was pulling off the biggest farce in history every time I got a job. To me, the privilege of selecting your work and portraying a world of glamour was reserved for the models with big profiles or rich parents, because even taking every job that came my way didn't amount to much in terms of my sporadic paycheques. Had I not stockpiled my income prior to this, I could never have afforded to indulge myself in this world of novelty work or keep at it long enough to start making some decent money from it.

In my experience, payment for jobs came in slowly and the odd payment just never arrived. There were occasions I chased a hundred quid for years. I would get a text to collect my envelope from the office – sometimes it contained a €500 cheque; a couple of months later it could be €1,500 and that would be a great day. It was all based on the agency's receipt of payment – there was no rhyme or reason to the system at the time and certainly no sense of stability. It was also extremely taboo within the industry to discuss the rate you were being paid directly with a client. Your agency told you the negotiated price and deducted their 20 per cent commission. With my burgeoning youthful freedom mostly dependent on these irregular payments and my new career now set in an industry that leaves you unsupervised and unaided in terms of managing your financial affairs, I did learn quickly to master routine saving and to keep a shrewd eye on every penny owed to me over long periods of time – two life skills I'm still grateful for and that are far more useful than being good at standing upright and walking in a straight line. But for every upside there comes a down.

In a legal sense, a model agency works for the model, taking their commission from the freelance bookings a model seeks out through days of unpaid castings and scheduled visits to a wide array of potential clients called 'go-sees'. As a model becomes better known and their regular client base and list of jobs grows, the castings and go-sees become less necessary, as they will be booked directly by name. The agency then justifies their commission by managing, negotiating and organising the model's bookings, making sure the jobs don't overlap or conflict and trying to secure the model the best fee for the work. They may also put a model forward for jobs if a client comes in search of a general look, potentially adding to a model's workload and increasing their income. Outside of this general understanding, there were no rules or regulations in the modelling industry when I started, no union or boards committed to protecting a model's rights, interests, wages, hours or working conditions. If you had an issue, you couldn't address it with your HR manager: you kept it to yourself or ran the risk of upsetting your agent with your whining and coincidently not booking any work for the following fortnight. Because in reality, models work for their agents and there was always another girl ready to take your job and not complain about it. This planted in me the seeds of scarcity and the pangs of competition. Over time, as well as trying to ensure that a liveable paycheque was on the horizon, being busy became directly linked to my feelings of success and stature. If I arrived on a weekday morning to film a fashion slot for *Ireland AM* and the other models were then running to a photocall that afternoon followed by a fashion show that evening while this was my only booking for the day, I would feel like crap.

And so began my long-winded, unconscious dance with ego.

CHAPTER 5

my first taste of travel

'I loved it all to the point of pain ... I wanted to see everything, go everywhere, never to return home ... [The trip] not only fed but gave focus to the restlessness I'd felt all my life. At last I had found a way to satisfy it, to meet it; at last I understood it. It had baffled and confounded me for years, the dissatisfaction, the constraint of the everyday, the tedium and scratchiness of routine, the irritating prickle of sameness ... [It] showed me that it was possible to ease this longing, to sate it. All I had to do was travel'

MAGGIE O'FARRELL

Joie de vivre, including that seductive, throaty French roll of the tongue, is the phrase I began to use to describe my first trip to Asia. Loosely translated it means 'the exuberant enjoyment of life' or 'the joy of everything'. I still remember the exact spine-tingling moment I felt it for the first time, in every cell of my body.

My legs were dangling over the bow of a wooden long-tail boat sailing at a steady pace over the small waves of the Andaman Sea. The old deck bounced, rhythmical and rattling, and the warm splash of tropical waters tickled my ankles. The sun was setting directly in front of our heading. All day the sky had been cerulean blue with a light speckling of pearly white, powdery clouds. But now the whole world had turned a glowing shade of pastel pink. During my portfolio preparation course for art college I had flicked through images of Monet's paintings while seeking inspiration, and I knew he had spent most of his life trying to capture the effects of changing light – painting the same scene at sunrise, midday, sunset and dusk. But never had I witnessed a scene so rife with colour and aliveness that it could have sparked such an obsession, until now. The horizon burned a rich shade of orange that melted into a mixture of radiating crimsons and gold, softening the skyline as I raised my eyes from the blinding sun. Directly above us, the sky was no longer blue; it was lavender with delicate streaks of blush and coral that deepened to a wine red when they sliced through a cloud.

A paper plate filled with boiled rice, grilled vegetables and freshly grilled fish, caught by our captain, warmed my thighs as the sea breeze tousled my long bleached-blonde hair, offering a cooling respite from the otherwise inescapable humidity. I don't know if it was my mindset or the perfect preparation of this simple local fare, but to this day I think it's one of the most delicious meals I've ever eaten. With a cool Chang beer in hand and this multihued performance playing out over the exotic landscape before me, I thought the moment couldn't get any more flawless – until I noticed a handful of eager early arrivals from the night sky who had to come to watch this spectacular display of transitory prowess. A few small sparkling stars pierced the blanket of twilight and the hint of a crescent moon loomed above, waiting patiently to take its place as nature's leading role. Neck strained fully back and eyes squinting to count the number of night-time visitors I could spot, my gaze was interrupted by two twinkling ropes of fairy lights onboard, switched on by the deckhand. Our rickety little boat with its flaking mint-green paint, colourful ribbons and flower garlands tied to the bow for good luck was now the most charming vessel on the sea. As if to make this moment as cliché as humanly possible, the deckhand then turned on All Saints' 'Pure Shores', the official soundtrack to the 2000 cult classic *The Beach*. The familiar harmony and everything it had come to represent for me after watching that movie maybe a hundred times made the hairs on the back of my neck stand up.

Hypnotised by the sounds of ambient, dreamy pop and fairy lights glinting on the currents, I hadn't noticed that my friend Steph had come to sit beside me until she pulled me out of my reverie with the words, 'We're nearly back.' She was pointing at our island home growing large on the horizon. It was rocky while at the same time lusciously green, and we were so close now that we could make out the palm-tree-fringed edge of the sandy stretch beside the wooden dock. Behind it the nightly hum and buzz of Phi Phi's only main street would be kicking off. The day itself had been pure magic, spent lazing on the iconic white sand of Maya Bay, our reclining only interrupted for dips in the perfectly clear, temperate waters or for strolls through the surrounding dense jungle flora, reminiscent of *Jurassic Park*. That evening we had plans to watch a fire performance on the beach before visiting every waterfront coconut hut turned cocktail hut. After dark people would spill from these bars onto the beach, buckets of drinks in hand, swaying to the muddled chorus of conflicting genres of music that blasted from all the establishments' competing speakers.

Sitting on that little boat on that beautiful evening in Thailand, I thought it might be impossible to feel any happier. I was exactly where I was meant to be and I knew it more profoundly than I'd ever known anything. I had never felt more alive. My heart raced and my cheeks flushed with the exhilaration of utter freedom: I had finally found it.

Aged 20, I had finally had my first experience of an unrivalled internal joy I would come to label my 'nature high'. A decade later, the deep yearning to relive this feeling would become my saviour.

∘ ∘ ∘

Up to that point I'd been on holidays with my family to Tipperary, Wexford, Kerry, the Isle of Man and the Costa del Sol. I'd once been allowed to join my cousin Niamh on a school trip to Pompeii because her mam, my auntie, was one of the teachers taking the group. The girls and I had also spent our week-long sixth-year holiday at our friend Amy's family holiday home in the Algarve. Privileged as I was to have enjoyed these getaways during my youth, I started to resent the dull mediocrity of my existence, overcome with an unquenchable thirst to get out and see the world. I was still wholeheartedly embracing the 'live for today' attitude. After modelling and waitressing for a year my savings had definitely stopped growing, but I had managed to live on my modest income without skimming too much from it. Budgets established, the girls and I started to discuss the idea of a proper adventure to somewhere far from home, where everything was different and we could broaden our perspectives ... I'm joking – we chose Thailand for the Full Moon Party.

The era of self-booked holidays was still emerging and we were far too inexperienced when it came to travel to trust our own judgement on where to go or what to do in such an alien place. Enlisting the help of a youth- and adventure-focused travel company in Dublin, we planned a three-and-a-half-week tour around Thailand that covered everything from the jungles of the north on the border with Laos to the chaos of Bangkok and the paradise islands of the south. There would be day-long bus journeys and overnight boats, tuk-tuks, elephants, temples and pad Thai from the source instead of the local takeaway. It all sounded so unfamiliar and thrilling

– we were sold. Orlaith, Steph, Ruth, Michelle, Niamh, Laura and I boarded our Thai Airways flight in the summer of 2008, and even that was enough to give me butterflies in my stomach. I must have said *sawadee ka*, the Thai word for hello, 10 times before even getting to my seat. I had learned it from a sheet of useful phrases that had been included with our ticket pack from the travel company and I felt like a real intrepid traveller bandying it about so casually. The flight was 14 hours, my first-ever long haul, and I was convinced it would be impossible to survive in a large flying Pringles tube for that length of time, so I had prepared with military precision. I had packed an elaborate and excessive array of snacks that had been cause for jeering from the girls prior to boarding. Well, that changed when, three-quarters of the way through the flight, we were offered a snack that looked like an innocent pot noodle, only to find it was filled with tiny octopus. My box of granola bars was swiftly passed among the group – intrepid traveller might have been a stretch.

The first two weeks of our trip were a whirlwind of new experiences and the most fun I had ever had. We explored the mountainous rainforests around Chiang Mai, helping elephants to bathe in a muddy stream and encountering the isolated inhabitants of various hill tribes in the region, getting to glimpse their unique dress and customs. At the time Chiang Mai didn't rate highly on the average backpacker's route, and the difficulty it took to get there didn't help, so it remained relatively disconnected from Westerners. I remember having a profound realisation at the time, one that was so simple and obvious yet had never occurred to me before then: that every one of the billions of people on this planet is living a life as complex as my own. No matter how dissimilar our circumstances, they, too, are consumed with their dreams, plans, friends, worries and routines, and each of them are connected to a thousand other lives that are equally complex, the majority of which I would never even know existed. For the first time, I saw my own existence on a macro scale and briefly grasped how absolutely insignificant I was. In a way it was an upsetting thought and simultaneously a humbling and liberating one. But then the reflective moment was brief and soon lost in the chatter of a busy young mind.

From Chiang Mai we travelled south to Krabi on Thailand's west coast, famed for its jagged, sheer limestone boulders covered in rainforest vegetation and its easy access to some of the most picturesque tropical islands on the planet. We took a boat to the island of Koh Phi Phi Don, where we stayed in hillside huts nestled in the jungle on stilts overlooking the backpacker's favourite, Ton Sai Beach, and the tiny village of Phi Phi itself. We drank rum from fresh coconuts, ate so many of the street vendor's Nutella–banana roti pancakes we could have been sick and got hand-poked bamboo-stick tattoos. We visited Monkey Beach and Koh Phi Phi Leh, home to the remarkable Maya Bay and Pileh Lagoon, a pristine inlet framed by hundred-metre-tall limestone cliffs and the clearest emerald green water imaginable, the origin of my *joie de vivre*. With rubble and rock still roped off in piles dotted around the island, we met locals who told us tales of their tsunami survival and what it had done to their families, businesses and homes. My understanding of the world was broadening by the day and I cherished every moment of it, the unquenchable thirst that had brought me here to see, do and know more only growing.

Back on the mainland, we travelled across the entire width of the country, marvelling at the vast national parks teeming with wildlife and thundering waterfalls, before arriving at the province of Surat Thani. This is the gateway to the Ang Thong National Marine Park in the Gulf of Thailand, where we would visit the islands of Koh Samui and our most anticipated stop on the trip: Koh Pha-ngan. Tickets in hand, we filed in a single line onto a large wooden overnight boat that would be the uncomfortably close sleeping quarters for far too many backpackers that night. By chance, I found myself in a prime spot beneath one of the few limp fans tumbling air across the sweltering travellers huddled below. Cool and surprisingly cosy, I was swayed to sleep by the currents. That would be the only night's rest I'd get for the coming days. At 6 a.m. the following morning we docked in Koh Pha-ngan – we had arrived at Thailand's most famed party island.

Every month Haad Rin Beach plays host to the island's Full Moon Party, a spectacle of fire, UV neon paint and unbridled adolescent pheromones. Backpackers descend in their thousands for a night of debauchery, made possible by Asia's generally loose adherence to rules and regulations of any kind. Buckets are the drink of choice for every reveller, sold at hundreds of wood-and-nail stands lining the streets and the beach. Each contains ice, a 300ml bottle of spirits, a can of mixer and M–150, the Thai version of Red Bull. I have vague memories of climbing to the top of some wavering, burning scaffolding with Orlaith and then standing on a bar counter in broad daylight the following morning spraying Niamh, who was threatening to pass out face down in the sand, with a hose. I had never been to a party like it and I'm so glad we made sure to milk every minute for what it was worth. I didn't know then that my wonderful days in Thailand were closing in on an awful end.

On our last morning on Koh Pha-ngan I woke with a terrible pain behind my eyes. It felt strange and unfamiliar, as did my body and mood overall. I put it down to having slept with my hair in a tight ponytail for the night and the lingering remnants of a hang-over from the Full Moon Party a couple of days earlier. I didn't have much time to contemplate – I had to get my backpack organised to catch a morning boat to the neighbouring island of Koh Samui. Packing was an unusual struggle. I tried to describe the sensation to Ruth, telling her it felt like my bones hurt as well as my eyes. By the time I stepped off the tuk-tuk at the harbour, I could barely stand. It felt as though with every passing minute a monumental amount of energy was being sucked from me. Slumped on the boat, my temperature skyrocketed as the most extreme bout of shaking, sweating and nausea I've ever experienced set in. I don't recall getting off the boat but I was definitely helped, if not carried. I probably should have gone straight to the hospital at that point, but I was so weak that I vaguely remember pleading with the girls to just get me to a bed – I desperately wanted sleep and solitude. Over the course of just a few hours, I had collapsed into the grip of a severe fever and I had no idea why. All I knew was that it hurt to turn my head, it hurt to open my eyes, it hurt to think. I had to rest urgently; I would figure it out in the morning.

But there was no morning, so to speak, as the days and nights of the coming week meshed into one long involuntary type of coma. It was as if my body shut down and went into hibernation against my will. I recall waking for brief intervals, bordering on delusional, the mattress soaked to capacity with my sweat. I never knew if it was day or night. The fatigue was so extraordinary and unbeatable – on one occasion I attempted a necessary yet arduous crawl to the toilet that resulted in a nap on the ground for a number of hours to generate enough strength to make it back into bed. My eyes throbbed to the point of blurred vision and my head pounded as if my brain was knocking off the solid surface of my skull. But I never once cried and I never once complained of feeling sick – I simply did not have the energy or bodily fluids to spare for either. The girls, who were sticking to our pre-planned itinerary of days packed with excursions, knew I was unwell; they would bring me water or a banana and ask how I was doing on their return in the evenings. 'Fine' would tumble from my chapped, dehydrated lips, a white lie in the hope they would leave as soon as possible so I could fall back into the safe depths of slumber, because even waking for those short, murky interactions was torturous. Every joint in my body ached so badly that I was almost immobile, and lifting my head from the pillow became inconceivable. I would later learn that this phase of the virus is commonly known as 'breakbone fever' and I can testify first hand that the moniker is absolutely merited.

I was obviously young and healthy, albeit regularly hung-over, before the onset of this sudden immune system crisis, so it took the guts of that full week of battling with the most aggressive fever I've ever encountered before my body started to follow suit and I looked as gravely ill as I felt. We were all young, naïve and entirely inexperienced when it came to how best to react in the face of a life-threatening tropical illness, but my friend Laura was the first to take some action. She insisted I get out of bed and have something to eat instead of settling for the two bites of banana I would generally agree to ingest while remaining horizontal in the evenings. She helped me up and tried to hold me upright on the short walk to the hotel's restaurant. It was only then that the drastic extent of my weight loss and general unravelling became apparent. For one thing, I stank, but what was even more concerning was that my previously skintight Juicy Couture tracksuit bottoms were now hanging loosely from my hip bones, with enough room for air to billow about inside the legs. I don't think I made it very far before my line of vision went white, soon followed by the unexpectedly delightful feeling of my body giving in to the overwhelming urge to collapse. I came round a few minutes later to a circle of human heads above my own. One of the Thai staff was frantically waving a mixture of strongly scented local pot-pourri beneath my nostrils while the girls, who were now freaked out by the rapid deterioration of my condition in this very foreign place, pleaded with me not to smell it. Impossible – it was so pungent I can still smell it today. Needless to say, I was finally bundled into a tuk-tuk and brought to the local hospital for a long-overdue assessment.

I had dengue fever – an acute virus transmitted through the bite of an infected mosquito. There are four closely related but distinct strains of the disease, all of which can progress to its most deadly expression, dengue haemorrhagic fever, if you're unlucky. But the really great news was that there was neither a vaccination nor a cure for the condition, so I just had to hope for the best and ride it out. Sent packing with a diagnosis of DENV–2, the medical jargon for the more virulent strain of the lot, I was given some Solpadeine and told to rest, take an effervescent vitamin C tablet every morning and drink lots of water. Maybe it was the miracle of Solpadeine or the natural course of things, but my fever did break that evening. Either way, I was relieved to be slowly released from its evil grasp.

I had three days left in Bangkok before my flight home – those were bed-bound but slightly more pleasant. I could eat a little and sit upright enough to enjoy the Thai sitcoms on our grainy hotel-room TV. Then on the day we were due to fly, I woke with a deep purple blood rash on my hands and feet. It was painful to touch or walk on, but until it inched its way up to my face, making me look undeniably infectious, I was getting on that plane. Dengue fever is not contagious, I would be hurting no one but myself and I'd wanted out of Thailand ever since I was coherent enough to be petrified.

By the time we landed in Dublin, the blood rash had spread as far as my knees and elbows. It was a solid plum colour that didn't dissipate or turn white when pressed. I had an idea at this point that the fever was only the beginning. My mam cried at the sight of me walking out of arrivals in my baggy tracksuit bottoms, gaunt and exhausted. I was so relieved to be home that I said nothing about the rash, foolishly hoping it would simply resolve itself and I could get on with my life now. In the car on the way home, I was banging on about the insatiable craving I had for a pint of milk while my mam googled the virus

I was playing host to. She cut me off mid-jabber, turning to me in the backseat to ask, 'Do you have a rash anywhere or have you had any nosebleeds?' Now this sounds like it's for dramatic effect, but those words had only left her mouth when the warm drops of blood began to fall from my nose onto those damn Juicy Couture tracksuit bottoms. Have I mentioned they were white?

As luck would have it, I had developed dengue haemorrhagic fever, the strain most likely to kill you as it rids your bloodstream of its much-needed white blood cells and platelets while wreaking havoc on your liver. I learned on arrival to the hospital that the blood rash I was hoping would heal itself was caused by my cell walls beginning to break down, leaking blood beneath my skin. This would be the worst-case scenario for my major organs too if I didn't receive swift medical intervention, so I was asked to report immediately if I began to bleed from my eyes, ears, gums or any other orifice. I told them that would be no problem; I'd let them know. I was quarantined in a room that looked like something straight off the set of *E.T.* It had an adjoining smaller room, about the size of your average toilet under the stairs, in which everyone had to dress themselves in a hair mask, face mask, apron, gloves and shoe covers prior to entering. On first sight of my visitors' mandatory attire, I thought I had been hugely mistaken prior to my flight and was, in fact, highly contagious. But without the protection of my old white blood cells, I was actually critically susceptible to any germs and the last thing my body needed, on top of trying to stop my organs from haemorrhaging, was a case of sepsis. We all have a natural clotting agent in our blood called platelets – mine were so low on admission that the nursing staff seemed to fear that I would accidently fall, graze my knee and bleed to death if I stepped out of bed, so as a result I had to call someone every time I needed to pee. For the first couple of weeks my blood pressure was so low that this didn't actually bother me – I was grateful for the help.

The four walls of the little *E.T.* hospital room became my whole world for a month, the days benchmarked by injections and meal deliveries. Every 12 hours on the dot, a gloopy concoction would be slowly administered through my IV cannula – I would feel it creep up my veins, cold and foreign, soon followed by the taste of metal before a strong urge to sleep. Every day the concoction would be tweaked and amended based on any positive reaction from my blood count or liver function, and with it I slowly began to regain my vitality and the general feeling of familiarity within my own body. I was beating the virus. But the doctor who visited me from the Tropical Medical Bureau warned me that I had been incredibly lucky and should now essentially dedicate the rest of my life to never contracting dengue fever again. Apparently I had immunity to whichever one of the four strains I had contracted, but re-exposure to the disease via another strain would mean almost certain redevelopment of dengue haemorrhagic fever, and there are not many studies of people who have survived it twice. The only way to be certain of never catching dengue fever again was to avoid all travel to Africa, Central and South America, the Caribbean, the Eastern Mediterranean and all of South East Asia – 'until perhaps one day a vaccination is developed', he'd offered as a slice of hope. As of today, there's still none. If his cautioning hadn't been enough to scare me into staying at home indefinitely, the lingering impact of beating the virus certainly was.

For a number of years after recovering from the initial infection, I battled recurring fevers, like an unceasing, unwelcome ripple of aftershocks. I had just turned 20 years old and was now basically confined to life in Ireland, yet I was informed that I also couldn't drink alcohol for the foreseeable future on account of the beating my liver had taken. 'Excuse me? What exactly do you suggest I do with my time, so?' was my baffled reaction. But that wasn't the worst of the news; my parents were also warned that occurrences of clinical depression had been correlated with the aftermath of severe cases of dengue. They kept that information from me so that I could be blissfully ignorant and without worry, which might sidestep any of my own contribution to its onset. Regardless of their best efforts, the months after leaving the hospital were far from my happiest.

My body remained so relentlessly skinny that I took to ordering butt pads and sticky chicken fillets for the inside of my bra from Amazon. I didn't feel anything like my healthier, curvier former self. And if that wasn't enough of an attack on my budding femininity, my hair began to fall out. As if to taunt me, it lay fully intact for nearly three months after my recovery and then suddenly began to evenly shed across my whole head. I wasn't sure what was happening at first – my hair had felt drier and more brittle than usual, but I could always put that down to my request to every hairdresser to make me 'as blonde as possible, please'. Within a week or so it became apparent that the amount of shedding was neither normal nor subsiding, as my scalp became visible through the thinning cover of hair. I couldn't take the slow and humiliating pace at which I was morphing into Gollum from *Lord of the Rings*, so I took a hair clippers and shaved my head to be done with it. This really was the virus that kept on giving, as a quick Google search revealed that this stage of the fun was called dengue-associated telogen effluvium, a type of temporary alopecia generally caused by medications, hormonal stress or severe systemic infections, all of which I had experienced in abundance over the previous half year. To add insult to injury, only the unluckiest of all dengue victims actually experience hair loss in the aftermath – it is quite rare, meaning I really did win the dengue lottery.

Considering the general trauma of the entire event, I was proud of my body. It had somehow known to salvage the maximum amount of energy to fight those invading foreign bodies, abandoning secondary non-life-giving processes, like hair growth, in favour of fuelling the operations more necessary for survival, like liver function. Ultimately, I mourned the loss of my ability to follow that compelling feeling of *joie de vivre* far more than the loss of the hair on my head. My new identity as a bleach-blonde pageant-queen wannabe turned commercial model was gone but, more achingly, so too was any prospect of experiencing the wonders I knew would come from long-term travel. With the worst of the ordeal raw in my memory, and in many ways still ongoing, I knew, too, that the level of fear now instilled in me meant most of the world truly was out of bounds.

I mourned all the places I'd never see, all the people I'd never meet and all the things I'd never learn. It felt as though I had no other option than to bury the dream and move on, and in a lot of ways I did concede defeat. My experience with dengue fever robbed me of an ability to choose where I travelled, but I recognised that I could still exert some control over my life. So, I decided I would try to find that same sense of aliveness at home. And with that, I began focusing my attentions fully on my career. But somewhere inside me there remained a quiet but deep-rooted inability to simply accept this life sentence – to accept that I would never again feel that freedom.

CHAPTER 6

my first love

'You are the finest, loveliest, tenderest, and most beautiful person I have ever known – and even that is an understatement'

F. SCOTT FITZGERALD

Before I met D, I had never been in love. With the exception of one or two teenage boyfriends and some short-lived non-committal romances, I had always been resoundingly single and very content with that. I wasn't much interested in meeting someone either. I didn't like the idea of having to compromise and consider, having to be held accountable or having someone to answer to. I was guarding my hard-earned independence and was fully focused on my career, which had become my defining attribute and the marker of my success and happiness in the world, especially in the absence of travel. Plus, based on my observations, relationships seemed to be a stressful hassle where you sort of hate the other person, but just not enough to leave them. All of this, on top of my subliminally held belief at the time that men were arseholes, had made me tough to tie down, to put it lightly.

After my hair fell out, I surrendered to an introverted ugly-duckling phase for a couple of years, which were void of dating. I point blank refused to let a scissors anywhere near my head once the temporary alopecia subsided, and as a result my hair bloomed into a very unflattering bulbous mushroom for far too long. On top of that, I opted to get train-track braces, including multiple mouth elastics that kind of locked my jaw, and I let my razor-thin, over-plucked eyebrows grow out in all their unkempt glory. Still, in spite of how I felt during this time, my short dark hair combined with my rail-thin frame ironically ended up turning me into what some might call a real model.

My drastic change of image was of unexpected interest to my agent, who felt it was a unique look on the Irish modelling scene, one that soon transitioned me from commercial work to editorial and catwalk. I started to book fashion shows with our most luxurious retailers and shoots with our most prolific photographers. In my wildest dreams, I had never thought I would be selected for this type of work – to me it was like an elite and aspirational secret club, one that I presumed was also the key to earning a proper living from modelling, so it was pretty disappointing to learn first hand that in reality, it paid even less and with much longer days than the cheesy commercial stuff. I had the privilege of sampling a wide variety of jobs over a number of years and although models' rates and rotas vary enormously I just couldn't see how I could sustain myself long-term in the industry in Ireland. I decided that my days dedicated to full-time modelling were numbered. I also hated how I looked, pale and gaunt with a muddy brown bowl on my head, but I tried to focus on those years as a sort of cocooning. I was biding my time, waiting to blossom back into myself, and I had big plans.

As soon as my hair reached that difficult length where the ends sat right between my earlobes and my jawline, when it could no longer be labelled a pixie cut but was still at least half a year's growth away from a bob, I booked myself in to get hair extensions. Long, thick locks cascaded from my head once more, the artificial ends lightened with blonde balayage, my own growth barely covering the bonds and far too short to blend naturally, but I didn't care. My sense of identity had become closely bound to being beautiful and not much else, and in my eyes I was finally starting to fit the bill again. But I wasn't done there; this was only the first of many flimsy plasters I would apply to the deep cracks in my confidence. I hired a sunbed, which I plugged into one of the power outlets in my house for daily use. I chose the fullest, lengthiest set of semi-permanent lashes on the menu. I got HD brows, long acrylic nails and fillers in my lips, long before Kylie Jenner made it as commonplace as a blow-dry. My newly established insecurities beamed from every uncharacteristically decorated inch of my face and body, and it didn't go unnoticed by the people closest to me. My 'look' prior to getting sick, if I had one at all, could have been best described as 'natural', if you wanted to be nice, or 'scruffy', if you wanted to be honest. For as long as I'd had autonomy over my own appearance, I had barely brushed my hair. But this was Daniella 2.0, the new me: professionally stunning.

Unaware of the irony, while still investing most of my energy into the reinvention of my appearance, I also decided that a career that depended entirely on something as fickle as my looks was too shallow for me. I would now set my sights on fulfilling my drama-school dreams of becoming a TV presenter. It was in alignment with the values I'd held so close since Kate's death: life is short, take the risk ... even if, again, you have no idea what you're doing and no one to ask how to do it. I had learned from my break into modelling that taking any assertive action in the direction you want to go will generally yield some results, or at the very least open some doors. So I began sending showreels to RTÉ and applying for any role on any show I heard about through the small number of contacts I had made while modelling, and that quickly created some opportunity. I secured a minor recurring role playing a complete lunatic in a number of comedy sketches filmed for RTÉ's *The Republic of Telly* and I was signed up as one of four models tasked with climbing to the summit of Kilimanjaro for charity in a four-part reality-TV-type documentary called *Catwalk to Kilimanjaro*. Not exactly the Louis Theroux-style serious investigative TV presenting I had envisioned, but a step in the right direction nonetheless.

By the time this opportunity presented itself it had been three years since my initial acute battle with dengue fever – after which a trip to Africa had seemed unthinkable. But the production was set to have a very quick turnaround of just seven days, during which I would face little to no exposure to mosquitos. We would go from the airplane to an air-conditioned van to a single overnight stay in a building with brick walls, sealed windows and mosquito nets over the beds. This would be a stark contrast to the huts I had been staying in in Thailand. For the first couple of hours on the first day of our hike I would have to ensure I wore full-length trousers, long sleeves and lots of repellent. I was so paranoid about any of my skin being exposed that I even covered my face with a repellent-soaked buff, but after the first day we would be climbing at an altitude at which there was no risk of infection because there weren't any mosquitos at all. I would have the same small window of risk on our descent and then it would be a quick repeat of our arrival, only this time in the direction of home.

It was a chance to conquer new heights and to get a small taste for travel again, while being a part of a show that might also help to advance my career. However, from the moment I stepped on to the plane in Dublin Airport I was awash with fear and anxiety that stayed with me – even in the safety of the high altitudes – until I was on the plane home. In many ways I treasured the experience but there was absolutely no sense of the freedom I had previously felt. I spent so much of my time fretting and berating myself for the decision that many times during the trip I asked myself if it was it worth it at all. Once home, I was in no rush to feel that way again anytime soon.

Nevertheless, with the opening of opportunities like this one, I was beginning to learn the value of contacts in a small city like Dublin, so I used this as my excuse to start going out a handful of nights a week – it was just an added bonus that I also got to exploit the generous table service the city's clubs afforded groups of models on the tear.

At this point I hadn't drunk in years, but with my new hair firmly glued in place I finally felt worthy of being seen in public again, and under the initial guise of networking I took to partying like it was a profession. All the typical mistakes and nights of regret I had managed to avoid thanks to my weak liver were then played out, condensed into just under a year that was only lightly speckled with sobriety. I had moved into a house in the city with Georgia Salpa, who was at the peak of her fame as a model in Ireland, and often riding the coat-tails of her hard-earned notoriety. When I wasn't in the Krystal nightclub penthouse, I was enjoying a glamorous girls' holiday in Marbella. It was an outrageous amount of fun, yet when I look back over my life so far, this is the version of myself I am least proud of, mostly because the difference between me and the other girls was that I didn't know when to stop.

When they would retire at a reasonable hour, I would not. I would go out three nights in a row instead of two. I couldn't count the number of times I ate an actual fry in Krystal in the unforgiving light of the following morning because the management had got to know me as one of the few stragglers who just wouldn't go home and probably thought it best to at least give me some sustenance from the adjoining hotel kitchen. I was always looking for the next party because I couldn't face the hang-over. Prior to my liver taking a beating I was an almighty lightweight, so with my ability to break down alcohol even further impaired I made some very questionable decisions over the course of that year – multiple short flings with multiple Irish rugby players being one. I'm sure my name was held in high regard among the relatively small squad.

During this period, if I'd spent a full day in bed, smoked a whole packet of cigarettes and ordered a beef and broccoli stir-fry with extra oyster sauce from the takeaway, I would have genuinely considered it to be a fairly health-conscious day of self-care – I mean, I ate broccoli! The one upside to this lifestyle was that I finally managed to overcome the enduring weight loss I'd been battling since contracting dengue fever three years earlier – I filled out quite considerably over the space of a few months. On the rare occasions I went home, my mother would tell me in no uncertain terms, 'Your skin looks like shit and your eye bags are nearly down to your chin.' One of the girls might also chime in with, 'How far has your head travelled up your arse now?' And neither of them was wrong. This is the only time in my life I pulled away from my friends and family, in both a physical and an emotional sense. They couldn't relate to the life I was living and I couldn't have cared less for a while. As far as I was concerned, I didn't ask for their constructive criticism. I was having a ball, even if I knew I'd lost touch with why I'd started going out in the first place.

Surprisingly enough, my youthful vigour did allow me to sometimes work through the haze of my hang-over and I continued to model sporadically, returning to my roots as a tabloid photo-call girl. During that messy year, I also somehow managed to secure the biggest TV presenting job I could have dreamed of booking. After testing for the role at a casting, I was selected to host an extreme sports series called *Bulletin TV* alongside Aidan Power that was scheduled to air on RTÉ2. The irony of how at odds my current lifestyle was with this role wasn't lost on me. It also occurred to me that not one of the people from the production company or the TV station who'd hired me had met me while scouting for talent in the Krystal penthouse in the early hours of the morning. At that point I probably should have reined it in and saved myself the headaches in the name of networking. But I couldn't. Getting shitfaced for most of the week had become part of who I was and, honestly, I enjoyed it too much. Not even achieving the kind of career progression that had started it all could now call time on my behaviour. No, that only happened after the single biggest regret of my life – one that meant I could no longer hide from the growing separation between who I thought I was and who I'd actually turned out to be.

On yet another typical night in Krystal, spent downing double vodkas and cranberry juice while dancing precariously in heels on whatever neutral-coloured furniture was in my vicinity, I heard a rumour at about 4 a.m. that Coppers was hosting a lock-in a few doors down. Overjoyed at the notion, I told the few people left with me at that hour that I would check it out and if the tales were true I'd be back to rally the troops for a roll-over spent raving to a medley of 5ive's greatest hits in our city's most beloved establishment. Once out on the quiet street, it became obvious that the rumour was not true and most people were winding down for the night, the area starting to clear. That familiar feeling of self-loathing began to creep up my spine as I quickened my pace back to the door of Krystal, but it was now locked, with no bouncer on duty. My repeated calls to my friends inside went unanswered and the night looked like it was set to come to an underwhelming and premature end, until he beckoned to me from the door of a crowded taxi.

I didn't know him well, just his name and the connection of a few mutual friends. I was also friendly with his girlfriend. We weren't particularly close but I was very fond of her – we had known each other for years and got on really well whenever we crossed paths. He told me he was having a house party and I was more than welcome. I tried to call upstairs to my friends a couple more times to no avail, and at this point I had kept a taxi of people who'd extended an invite to me waiting for longer than was socially acceptable. Mistake number one: being so eager to continue the session that you'd rather drive 30 minutes out of the city with a car full of people you don't know rather than go home and accept that tomorrow is another day.

I won't drag you through a prolonged explanation to get to mistake number two: we slept together that night. An intimate interaction that sits in a void in my memory, but I know it happened because I woke half-dressed in his bed. I have no doubt I played a role in its unfolding – I would be lying if I didn't admit I thought he was very attractive and I was clearly in a state where my inhibitions, my values and my regard for others had become irrelevant. My memory of the house party is faint, to say the least, with the exception of one vivid moment when he insisted I try a spoonful of his homemade brown-bread ice cream. There was nothing more sinister to this, in case you're wondering, just a man who was genuinely proud of his work and me no doubt basking in the attention of being his selected food critic. But in the stark, awful light of the next morning, I have never disliked myself so much.

I took the longest taxi drive of my life back to the city and landed on the doorstep of my friend Claire's house, where any act of togetherness I had managed to pull off since opening my eyes broke with the weight of my own guilt. She did as all good friends would do, offering the few words she could to reassure and uplift me – 'we all make mistakes' – trying her best to right all my wrongs with a cup of Barry's tea. But we both knew I had crossed a line that should never be crossed. I was no longer the girl's girl I had taken such pride in being. In fact, I was barely even a friend to any of my girls from school any more, and I hadn't been since I'd moved to Dublin and got swept up in becoming something or someone. I had drifted far, far away from who I was and where I came from. The fear was so considerable that, swaddled in a blanket on Claire's couch, I booked the next available one-way ticket to Portugal, leaving the following morning. Mistake number three: still practising the art of complete avoidance in difficult situations.

I handled the aftermath like a coward. With Dublin being about the size of a large village, I knew it would be only a matter of time until the truth came out, and when it did I simply refused to answer my phone, safe in the Algarve like a fleeing criminal. My friend was rightfully enraged by the betrayal and no doubt even more triggered by my adamant refusal to respond to her persistent calls, denying her even a crumb of explanation or an outlet for her hurt. Instead of facing what I had done, accepting the consequences and apologising sincerely and profusely, I let the fear of owning up hijack my better judgement in the hopes it would all just disappear. But of course it didn't, and my reputation took a hammering in some of Dublin's social circles in the weeks that followed, fuelled by rumours that I was host to more than one STI and a vagina that was fairly unsavoury to the eye, among other things. I was distraught, not because of the shrapnel I was facing from my own bad choices, but because I had truly hurt someone I liked a lot, ultimately losing her friendship and, indirectly, the friendship of many others connected to us both who would easily pick their side in the most clear-cut clash in history.

Much to my despair, I was forced home from Portugal because I had to work to keep myself alive, although I did seriously contemplate packing it all in to live on a remote beach where I would learn to spear-fish and forage in nature. But as well as filming for *Bulletin TV*, prior to this mess I had committed to working on an online series interviewing musicians at one of Ireland's biggest festivals.

D was in a band, and the first time we met and spoke properly was when I interviewed him as part of this job. He was also a popular radio presenter on Spin 103.8, the station I had so proudly represented in the Miss Ireland pageant some years earlier, so we knew of each other from a distance, but on meeting there was an unexpected yet undeniable spark. Unexpected because he couldn't have been further from my usual preference, which up to that point had been the muscular, sallow-skinned, sandy-haired, private-schooled, dim-yet-arrogant, emotionally unavailable type. Even better if they were also outright mean, had commitment issues and/or sent me mixed signals over a long period of my invested time. D was the opposite of this in every way – thin and tall, with dark floppy hair, pale skin and a dress sense that was undeniably emo. On first impression, he was also quick-witted, humble and unusually aware of his own feelings. He had a kind, soft face and a quirky sort of self-assuredness that felt rooted in an innate decency.

I didn't notice that after our meeting I began to trade getting ready for nights out for sitting in to stream the live feed of his weekday evening radio show on the station's website until Georgia pointed it out to me. 'I think you like him – you're literally creeping on him in work every day of the week.' She was right, I did. He felt magnetic to me and I wanted to get to know him better, so I took an opportunity to insert myself into a competition he was part of. The marketing department of the radio station had entered him in a teen magazine's search for Ireland's Bachelor of the Year, a clever ploy to attract new young listeners who might then become loyal fans of the show on account of D and his co-host's boyish charm, as well as the prospect of winning some Justin Bieber concert tickets. I made him a T-shirt to wear on the night of the final that read 'Will anyone date D?' in handwritten marker. It came down to reader votes and, devastatingly, he didn't win, but I was there as emotional support and we had our first kiss instead.

I was 23, and I had never known a love like the love D showed me every day after that for the following four years. I thought it was supposed to feel like losing yourself to madness, but instead it was restful, a slow and steady stream of trust, respect and contentment. I was always convinced it was too good to be true, waiting for the veil of niceness to drop so I could revel in the 'told you so'. He was the most calming, centring and caring person to ever enter my life, and I couldn't have needed him more at that time. He pulled me right back to earth, got me refocused on my career and showed up for me every single day with unconditional love, support, guidance and an unshakable kindness. He was straightforward and reliable, overflowing with integrity and always true to his word.

When I realised I was falling in love with him I tried over and over to push him away. I was sure there was no way he could be this kind, this smart, this funny, this loving and this effortless – there had to be a catch and I didn't want to find out what it was after I'd caught feelings. But he would consistently react to my regular destructive tantrums and varying-degree mood swings with the perfect balance of distance and gentleness. It was like, without any need for explanation, he understood my brokenness and my strange attachment to my independence. Like an adoring audience, he let me be entirely myself and told me it was perfect. At the end of the day, with my make-up off, my hair scraped up in a messy bun and my legs in need of a shave draped over his, he would announce how beautiful he thought I was. He made me feel so safe and so worthy that, slowly but surely, I began to ease up on the fake lashes, the fake nails and the fake tan. Within months of meeting him it was all gone, even the hair extensions. I would get butterflies in my stomach every Friday at the thought of spending the weekend together, and I became convinced that he had assigned himself the mission of making me laugh every day. When I quizzed him on that, he responded with, 'I'm just happiest when you're happy.'

Are you nauseated by all of this yet? Because there's more …

When the TV show I was working on wasn't recommissioned, he offered to help me move into radio presenting instead, a potentially more reliable source of broadcasting work if I was any good at it. I remember the first time I sat in the studio to watch him panel his show. In front of him were two large desks filled with faders, buttons, knobs and flashing lights; behind the desks were four computer screens with what looked to me like matrix code flowing through them. He was rapidly manipulating one desk with his left hand and the other with his right while also producing an array of perfectly timed sound effects from a smaller keyboard in the middle. On top of this, he was monitoring the four ever-changing screens, pre-recording and editing segments for the show during songs and managing multiple callers for various competitions. I thought it was probably more convoluted than brain surgery and became resigned to the fact that in a million lifetimes I could never master this kind of multitasking ability while also delivering an entertaining live radio show. But with privileged access to the impressive well of his knowledge and skill in the area, I quickly learned the technical basics – things like how to edit audio and construct a link – and eventually even started panelling those desks. I was learning and growing, with a focus I hadn't had in years.

But there was one small problem: every time the studio microphone would turn on, accompanied by that bright-red On Air sign, my mouth would go dry, my heart would race uncomfortably fast and I would become noticeably breathless within seconds. I would start stumbling over words, panic and either end the link abruptly or lose my train of thought and sort of babble nonsense into a song. There was no obvious sparkle of promise about my first attempts at radio.

Still, D encouraged me to challenge myself with some discipline and commit to practising my new skill, so I took on hosting my own show a number of evenings a week on a voluntary digital station used to train new presenters. It was an added perk that the small studio I would be using was in the same building as his. I was still taking on all the modelling jobs I could and occasionally working in TV, so when he knew I'd had a long day before coming in to the station, he would sometimes leave a cup of tea or some salad on my desk, other times flowers or an encouraging note. One particular day, he left a very large Easter egg accompanied by a personalised note from the Easter bunny herself, which read, 'I gave birth to this, through my vagina. Happy Easter X.'

Whether it was in work or in our day-to-day life, he made everything better, his love and support apparent, thoughtful and steady at all times. I began to flourish in a way I hadn't since before I'd got sick all those years ago. Failing didn't seem quite as scary when I knew he was there to catch me. I felt more settled and more seen than ever before, and for a long time I was the happiest I had ever been too.

CHAPTER 7

success and influence(r)

'Pain that is not transformed
will always be transmitted'

RICHARD ROHR

22 November 2016, 2.44 a.m.

Be kind and patient every day.

Be thoughtful and compassionate.

Be supportive, always.

Make an effort with family and friends, and the hobbies and interests that make their eyes light up.

Make time for more self-care – my own happiness is important for the benefit of the relationship.

These are the revelations I recorded on my Notes app in the early hours one morning after my relationship with D ended. I can still remember the moment this modest and long-overdue swell of self-reflection came over me, like I'd stumbled upon some profound epiphany on how to love. It seems some people are born with an instinctive ability to function optimally in romantic relationships, but as is probably clear from these worryingly elemental insights, some aren't. Or perhaps we never learn, forget how or are scared to as a result of our life experiences. It was actually weeks and weeks of relentless crying that finally brought me to this brief moment of introspection – and when I say relentless, I mean it.

The only time I stopped sobbing was between the weekday hours of 6.45 a.m. to 9.45 a.m., and only because it would have been a real hindrance for my co-host Cormac and me to get through our breakfast radio show otherwise. That said, there was a period where I did such a poor job of holding it together for even that small window of time that the very sweet presenter of the show after ours actually bought me a small guardian-angel lapel pin 'to watch over me'. I think she may have felt compelled to do so after the day we were forced to load extra songs into the show's playlist to allow me blocks of time between live links where I could crumble into convulsions, which I would then unconvincingly try to blame on the announcement of Trump's election, among other things.

I was a very tender woman on the edge. On a regular day, I would start to cry as soon as I woke up and reality began to reassemble from the hazy hiatus of sleep. I'd continue crying under the cover of the night sky on my cycle in to the studio, force myself to stop when I wasn't in a toilet cubicle during working hours, hold in the tears with maximum effort on my cycle home, only because witnessing a woman wailing through town on her bike is probably a little unsettling, then start sobbing again the moment the lift doors closed in my apartment building and go on to cry for the evening with varying degrees of intensity until I cried myself to sleep. A remotely melancholy key in any song set me off, TV shows and commercials with any heightened emotion set me off, the internet in general set me off, books set me off, the mere sight of couples, old people and puppies set me off. Everything seemed to trigger the tears. In fact, the urge to cry at all times was so overwhelming that I booked myself in to speak with a counsellor. I figured this was the only answer, as it was becoming debilitating in my daily life.

But waiting in the lobby for our first meeting, I cried because D's radio show was playing over the speakers. Then inside the sanctuary of the counsellor's room, when asked to make a list of all the reasons D wasn't right for me, I cried again because I couldn't think of any that weren't ridiculous.

The truth is that D was perfectly right and even then I knew it had been a privilege to have him in my life for so long. It was me that was the problem, and in hindsight I was only at the very, very beginning of fully grasping that fact. But one nugget of wisdom did stay with me from that single desperate counselling session – it was what the counsellor offered as the possible reason for my inability to stop crying as well as the feelings I was expressing to him about how I had acted in the relationship.

'If it's hysterical, it's historical. If you're acting out of character, that's because somewhere in your life the relationship with yourself or with someone else was damaged, and now you're feeling triggered by that damage in a new situation. You need to follow the breadcrumbs back to that initial relationship, do the work and start to heal.'

I hadn't a clue what he was talking about, so I labelled it as some woo-woo notion lacking in any scientific basis or evidence, paid him his 80 quid and left. At the time, I wasn't remotely spiritual or mindful: I was a woman who dealt only in what I considered to be facts. I wanted straight answers and immediate remedies, not vague time-wasting deep-dives into my psyche. What I did know was that, metaphorically, most break-ups can be best described as: you have a very best friend in the world and then they essentially die. Except on this occasion it was worse, because in the aftermath of the break-up I couldn't shake the feeling that I'd actually slowly tortured my best friend to death.

The tears kept coming because, once the dust settled and the loss set in, I knew I hadn't treated the relationship with the respect or value it had deserved, nor had I left it with grace. I hadn't been kind or patient; I'd been mostly angry and inconsiderate. I hadn't been thoughtful or compassionate either; in fact, I'd been a vacuum for those entitlements, which flowed almost always in one direction, from him to me, and were absorbed rather than reciprocated. On top of that, I was starting to recognise that I hadn't been at all supportive, nurturing, willing to compromise or interested in making any real effort when it came to his family, friends or hobbies. It goes without saying that we shared a lot of love and good times over the four years we spent together, but I had acted selfishly far too much of the time, as if the relationship existed solely to serve me. And to make it worse, D had offered all of the above, unconditionally and in bucket loads.

I now felt that he had endured being a dumping ground for all my daily anger, stress and worry, and not once had I stopped to assess or take responsibility for the energy I brought into his life every day – maybe because he never complained.

What was causing me so much pain was that I couldn't reconcile what I was realising with another belief I simultaneously held about myself: that I was a nice, kind and sensitive person. How and why had I acted the opposite for so long to the one person who had shown me nothing but the most unconditional love anyone could ever hope to find? I had also been certain for our entire relationship that I didn't need D – I was fine on my own. So why was I so far from fine now that he was gone?

The answer to these questions would require some real self-awareness and acquiring that self-awareness would require time and deep reflection. So I ensured I was far too busy to find that time.

And instead I cried ...

° ° °

My first job in radio was the overnight weekday shift on midlands iRadio. The station's management heard my Bambi-legged presenting on that voluntary digital station D had encouraged me to practise on and decided to take a shot on me, pairing me with a long-time station contributor and comedian called Cormac. On the first link of our first live show, we didn't push up the correct faders and so no audio aired. A listener would have heard nothing but the faint elevator music that generally underlies a presenter's chatter for three whole minutes. We also took the station off air more than once by going to make cups of tea while playing a pre-recorded interview we thought we had set to seamlessly run into the next song. We'd come back into the studio to find multiple missed calls from our boss and absolute silence on air – once for over eight minutes. I think the only reason they didn't sack us is because we had a genuinely rare chemistry for a manufactured pairing. To this day, no one has made me belly laugh like Cormac did almost every day of the two and a half years we worked as radio husband and wife. On air, we were light-hearted, upbeat and fun. Off air, I spent a whole lot of my time being a far cry from that.

Our studio was on the far side of Athlone and I would commute every day from Kildare for the show, a three-hour round trip – I had moved home to my parents' house in an attempt to find a middle ground for my daily work commitments in Dublin and Westmeath. We'd wrap at midnight and every single night D would chat to me over the car speaker until I pulled into my driveway to make sure I got home safely. I generally spent the hour and a half moaning about the length of the drive or whatever else had irked me that day. At the time I was not naturally inclined to look on the bright side, and one topic I loved to hammer home repeatedly was my feelings about Angela Scanlon.

Even though I had moved into radio presenting I was still actively pursuing TV work, which, in spite of being far less well paid, I still considered the more impressive of the two mediums. I harboured dreams of becoming the Irish Louis Theroux, even though I had little to no life experience, no third-level education and no notable area of expertise outside of wearing a bikini on Grafton Street. Prior to my first offer of a job in radio, while still learning the ropes on the voluntary station, I had been working with Angela on a TV show that was cancelled mid-season. In the aftermath, we had both made a pitch to bag a one-hour documentary to be aired on RTÉ2. Considering her impressive and ongoing presenting career, it's obvious now why she nailed the gig and turned that shot at a one-hour doc into multiple follow-up series. But I just couldn't fathom the rejection. I now sort of admire that level of blind, dogged ambition – I mean, in my mind there was no reason for RTÉ not to commission my documentary pitch about fathers who symbolically marry their daughters to bind them to their virginity in the American Bible Belt. But then, everything was justification to burn D's ears off with my whining – her getting the job, the build-up to her show being aired, the success of her show, her ever-growing list of follow-up shows ... None of it had anything to do with me, of course, yet I couldn't have taken it all more personally or let it affect my mood more, mostly to the detriment of D's day. I was so blinded by what I didn't have, I couldn't enjoy what I did.

After just six months on the overnight shift in iRadio, Cormac and I were offered an evening weekday chart show on the radio station I had listened to my entire youth: Spin 103.8. In a twist of fate, or perhaps reaping the fruits of my labour, I would now be hosting the exact show I had watched D panel in awe and disbelief many years earlier. On the first day of our new show, D left a large bouquet of flowers and a bottle of prosecco on my desk for some post-broadcast celebrations. In spite of all I had to be grateful for, I'm sure I still found some way of linking Angela to the event and moaning for hours at how unfair the world was. I'm still not sure if I'd just become a career-obsessed nightmare of epic proportions with delusions of competitive scarcity or if I simply amplified those natural negative tendencies as part of my unconscious need to keep pushing D away. Maybe it was both.

Either way, despite my personal shortcomings, the trajectory of my professional life kept advancing and with it came another promotion. After a stint working the evening chart show that was as short as the night shift we'd filled before it, Cormac and I were offered the opportunity to take over as Spin 103.8's breakfast-show hosts, a prized role at the station's helm. I immediately let it be known that I didn't care for mornings and was very comfortable with my cushy evening slot. Maintaining that outwardly nonchalant stance on the offer, I realised while signing on the dotted line of my breakfast-show contract that it was the first time I'd managed to negotiate and secure a financially successful position since I'd stepped into the world of the self-employed at the tender age of 17. I was now 26. I had a brilliant, somewhat scarce and aspirational job and I was in a long-term, healthy (for one of us, at least) relationship with a man who made me feel adored every single day. Surely I was happy? At that point I was perhaps validated enough professionally – at least, enough to let my vendetta against Angela Scanlon go! – but on a personal level, of course I wasn't. External gains don't appease a discontented mind – although they certainly aided my desperate attempts to continue ignoring mine.

This advance into early morning broadcasting also quickly brought me to the point of having everything I thought I'd ever wanted, all of the 'I'll be happy when's. I thought I'd be happy when I moved back into the city from my parents' house in Kildare, but when my new salary afforded me a room in a penthouse apartment in Dublin 8 with two of my best friends, I could still find things to complain about. The traffic outside was too loud, my room was too hot and the electric blinds on our windows lowered too slowly, among other devastating daily burdens.

Then, once I owned a brand new car I'd be happy, right? Well, I went one better than that. My new position in Irish media gave me the opportunity to become an ambassador for Volkswagen Ireland, which meant my brand new Golf R-Line was updated every six months with a custom interior and my choice of paint colour and alloys. I didn't have to worry about the inconvenience of annual tax or insurance either – all I had to concern myself with was the privilege of driving it in exchange for a couple of Instagram posts and an appearance at an event or two where there was always free champagne. The novelty wore off so quickly that I felt absolutely nothing at all when I backed the car into a large cement pillar in my underground car park, no doubt due to an all-consuming distracted state about something ridiculous. I would arrive into work every morning to a stack of PR boxes containing an array of different gifts and invites, and the act of going through it all would actually annoy me, as would deciding where to put it all in my bedroom, which was already a cluttered mess of unnecessary crap.

Next, for all my adult years I had believed that my ultimate happiness lay in finding myself booked and busy to within an inch of my life. The scarcity of work had been deeply engrained in me after modelling and grasping for jobs in TV for nearly a decade, and I badly wanted to become a savvy, successful woman with a full schedule. Well, I would get it when, alongside presenting my breakfast radio show and modelling regularly, writing a monthly column for a glossy magazine and a weekly full-page spread for a tabloid newspaper, I was also swept up in a new-age career of sorts that would come to be labelled 'influencing'. I booked multiple campaigns and ambassador roles for a bunch of brands that all ran parallel. At one point I was the face of Vichy skincare, Cleanmarine krill oil supplements for PMS, Lipton Tea and an indoor-plant incentive by Bord na Móna while also promoting PrettyLittleThing clothing, Magnum ice cream, Lucozade Energy, Dolmio pasta and ProperCorn healthy popcorn to a lesser capacity every other day. I must have been a decent vessel for flogging food online. On top of all this, I was also booking MC gigs for large events, getting the opportunity to be on the cover of my favourite childhood magazines and, most surprisingly of all, couldn't keep up with the number of brands booking me to play two-hour DJ sets at their various launches and events. I never tried to become a DJ – people just started to call me one because I worked in radio and, all on its own, it grew legs until I was moonlighting as one, charging €1,000 for a two-hour set.

Speaking of money, I also thought I'd be happy when I was financially stable and free from living from sporadic paycheque to sporadic paycheque. Staying true to the girl I had been when I'd worked in the Meteor store in Newbridge during the day and the restaurant during the night, I was still an avid saver, even stricter now after years of modelling for breadcrumbs. I checked my bank account one day to find I had €120,000 when I compiled everything from my various savings accounts with my current account. I hadn't noticed any milestone because I was too busy working morning, noon and night every day of the week to amass that figure.

At that point, my relationship with D was on its last legs. He'd played second fiddle to my career and my perpetual bad mood for a long time, so I could reach the successes I once thought I'd only ever dream of, yet they weren't paying off in the ways I'd assumed they would. Where was the absorbing happiness that was to just come upon me one day in light of some final achievement? All I felt was chronic exhaustion and a general hum of unease. I was always rushing to leave one job early to arrive to the next one late, and in the process I was skimping on the most important relationships in my life, including the one with myself. But I was invested in being a highly competent person, so I ignored the whispers inside me that something felt a little off and continued my blind search for happiness in senseless productivity.

I set my sights on what I felt was my most worthy goal yet and a certain gateway to that elusive contentment others seemed to have found. I wanted to achieve recognition from my peers in broadcasting. I was a female anchor on a breakfast show, a rare enough phenomenon, and I thought an industry award and the associated recognition would induct me into a world of purpose and fulfilment. I got the nod that year as the only woman to make it onto the shortlist of the top five broadcasters in the country, all vying for the Broadcaster of the Year Award. I lost out on the award to D. We had split just a few weeks earlier and the ceremony took place in the midst of my crying phase, so perhaps it makes sense why it ultimately meant very little to me on the night.

o o o

I choose to reveal the above about my professional life not to brag or because I consider it to be the pinnacle of success, but because even doing and having more than I ever thought I could didn't make me happy for any notable duration. I was trying to fix or maybe avoid a broken part of myself by chasing love, approval, success or the million other things we seek for fulfilment outside ourselves. But no matter how much I got, until I realised who I was and made peace with it, I felt estranged from and unsettled in myself.

There's a Banksy quote I really like and have since come to live by: 'When the time comes to leave, just walk away quietly and don't make any fuss.' I couldn't have ended my relationship with D any further from this. I dragged him through months of my own uncertain back and forth, with no regard for how it must have affected his wellbeing. But we are the stories we tell ourselves and we can shape how we see the world with our selected beliefs, and I just wasn't ready to sit and read my own story. So instead I convinced myself that I was too full of life to be half-loved. The mind really is a powerful tool if I could use it to make me believe that D didn't love me enough, but that's what I did for a time. Love scared the hell out of me. Yes, in a good relationship you're safer with that person than with anyone else, but you're also more vulnerable to that person than to anyone else. That seemed to be an unavoidable part of being in love and I didn't like that paradox. I'd never learned to be vulnerable to a man, I'd never learned to communicate in a healthy way with a man and I'd certainly never learned how to love a man. I couldn't truly open myself up and allow D in. In spite of his years of love-laced effort, it's obvious to me now that no one can fix anyone else's shortcomings and, more than that, a person is unlikely to even begin to acknowledge any need for personal change until they themselves are good and ready. Or, like in my case, until they've run themselves into the ground with their own destructive behaviours.

When anger and hurt simmer inside of us, for any reasons, acknowledged or not, no relationship, no success, nothing at all in this world outside of ourselves will mask it or mend it for long. When I met D I didn't know myself, I didn't see my shortcomings, I didn't have a clue that I was angry or hurt. And after a couple of years in the safety of our relationship, I assumed that meeting someone like him was commonplace; my inexperience in long-term dating fooled me into thinking that everyone's default nature was to be kind and loving beyond measure, that everyone came with honesty, loyalty and integrity inbuilt. Somewhere along the way, his humility and humour got boring, his persistent positivity a pain in the face of my undulating moods. I don't think I ever fully valued the relationship and as my career blossomed I grew to disregard it further. Work and success were my primary concerns, the defining strings to my bow, and everything else, including D, was disposable. The fact is I didn't deserve D or the love he gave me for so many years, but without them, I don't know if I ever would have come to see my own flaws so undeniably.

He was the first man to teach me how to love and I am a better person now for simply having known him.

CHAPTER 8

uganda

Listen to the mustn'ts, child,
Listen to the don'ts
Listen to the shouldn'ts
The impossibles, the won'ts
Listen to the never haves
Then listen close to me –
Anything can happen, child,
Anything can be.

'Listen to the Mustn'ts'
SHEL SILVERSTEIN

The end of my relationship with D was also the beginning of the end of my ability to maintain a stable emotional state. My mental health declined fairly rapidly over the next six months, but in my ignorance I went out kicking and screaming, holding onto the life I'd built but could no longer live with every ounce of willpower in me.

I was single for less than a month when I met a man who couldn't have been more different from D in every way. To me, he was confident almost bordering on cocky, eccentric, chaotic, commanding and incredibly exciting compared to the stable sort of normality I had become so bored of. A handsome, rugged and regarded artist, he was larger than life and so accustomed to attention from women that I couldn't believe it when he focused his own on me. He enthralled me from the moment we met and I couldn't have willingly hopped into the front seat of our roller-coaster ride any faster.

The relationship was short but intense. As a person who had always taken great pride in my independence, this was my first taste of involuntary codependence, something I found confusing and overwhelming in good and bad ways. On the one hand, I thought this must be what real love felt like and I had just never known it until now, while on the other hand, I felt so out of control and unlike myself it was almost scary. I was completely addicted to him, to the point that any time apart would make me tense and uneasy. From the moment we met, everything that fell outside of our relationship, like my hobbies or interests or even my work, started to become a time-stealing hindrance. The defining factor of my every day was his mood – how he felt was how I felt, such was the level of my entwinement. Our highs were the highest I've ever been, but so, too, were the depths of our all-too-regular lows, which mostly came about because of the endless insecurity between us. It was emotional anarchy from day one. As you can imagine, this was a fairly all-consuming state of affairs and a convenient bypass of the brief but unpleasant self-reflection I had begun in the aftermath of my previous relationship. We were impractically head-over-heels and I was more than happy to distract myself with all of our unrealistic potential.

His work took him abroad on occasion, and such was the level of my obsession, I didn't hesitate when he asked me to travel with him to Uganda to help with a project he was to oversee in the world's largest refugee camp. It had been over 10 years since I had travelled to any country with a significant risk of dengue fever, with the exception of that one short and safe trip to Kilimanjaro, yet here I was headed straight to the heartland of the virus to pick up a paintbrush in camp Bidi Bidi, a settlement on a large stretch of remote dirt land in northern Uganda, on the border of the Congo and South Sudan. We would be staying in the nearby village of Yumbe for two weeks while we redesigned and painted a mud, brick and tin structure with holes for windows that had been masquerading as a school inside the camp for the ever-growing community of unaccompanied refugee children spilling over the border from South Sudan.

Before leaving, I hadn't thought much about the reality of what we were embarking on – the whole trip just seemed like a fairy-tale adventure, an extension of the romance novel I had found myself in in my mind. Considering that this was also my first truly foreign trip in a decade, the scenes on arrival were enough to knock some sense of real human suffering into my airy-fairy, self-absorbed head. The camp had been originally set up to accommodate 50,000 refugees, but by the time we visited, not long after its opening, there were just under 300,000 men, women and children trying to survive there. I say men, women and children when, in fact, well over half of the camp's occupants were unaccompanied minors whose parents had been lost or murdered in the gruesome ongoing civil war in South Sudan.

I had never seen anything like it. People queued for miles to collect a single bag of grain from the overtaxed and under-resourced workers representing a humanitarian organisation. A functioning water pump was a rare and precious find and the African heat was truly sweltering.

Mosquitos loomed low and thick above the barren, scorched red earth, and as we drove over the bumpy apex of a hill at the camp's entrance, through the haze there lay a vast shantytown, made of UN tarp and discarded wood, as far as the eye could see. When our aid-worker guide told us the camp spread 'further than the distance from Dublin to Galway', the scale of the crisis suddenly had a reference that I could wrap my head around. It was the size of a large cosmopolitan city built with nothing but sheer desperation by a frightened, fleeing nation who had lost everything but the clothes on their backs. Nobody should be able to survive like this for an extended period, traumatised by war and loss, with no proper shelter from the extremes of the heat and cold, no sanitation, no guarantee of fresh water to drink for days on end and limited access to any nutritious food, but somehow they were, even the tiny children who found themselves there alone, swept up in a frantic crowd.

It blew my mind that a humanitarian disaster of this magnitude could be taking place in the world and yet we go about our days entirely ignorant to it, fussing over some first-world stress. If it had been mentioned on the news at all I had missed it, even though part of my job on the breakfast show was to cue the news bulletins, on the hour, every morning of the week. Whether I cared or not, I could tell you what Kylie Jenner cooked for dinner or whether or not Justin Bieber was single, but I had heard nothing at all about this. How can we form a well-rounded, informed view of the world and our place in it if we are only aware of a microscopic fraction of what's happening? In the midst of all the hysteria and passion playing out in my life, the endless working days and short sleepless nights, this trip to Uganda jolted me out of the depths of my own head and into a brief but enlightening macro view of what it means to live on this planet. I had fallen into arrogantly presuming my life should be special and happy, and when it wasn't I felt hard done by. But lying in my bed on the first night of our trip, forced to think through that day's short encounter with such senseless hardship, it dawned on me that this default inner narrative was deeply flawed. Winning a geographical lottery at birth was the only reason I was in this warm, safe room rather than lying cold, hungry and burdened with grief out there on the rocky earth.

Over the next fortnight we worked with hundreds of children from this makeshift community to paint their school in bright geometric shapes. The building sat slightly elevated and in a circular clearing used as a playground, where the students ran with rubber tyres twirled on sticks or made sculptures from the rubble and stones that littered the ground. It was the only splash of colour for miles and it could be seen from all angles in every direction – it felt like we were creating a little symbol of hope in a sea of desolation, and the children's constant excitement at our presence in the camp reinforced that. The days were long, hot and draining, but we would arrive having had a good night's sleep and some toast and jam for breakfast; we'd have rice and beans for lunch and access to bottled water and a fresh mango if we needed it during the day. However, the kids who worked just as hard as us for just as long arrived ready to go on empty stomachs, in yesterday's paint-stained and ripped clothes, and they didn't eat or drink a drop of water all day. We couldn't share our food or water with them, under orders from the local aid workers, or we would 'cause pandemonium'.

At the end of each day, we'd help the aid workers to share a small allocation of daily water from a number of jerry cans they'd stored away safely among the hundreds of children who would gather around us. With just a handful of cups to drink from, they would form long, patient queues in the hopes of a single sip. Some children would make it to the top of the queue and, instead of taking that much-needed water for themselves, would sacrifice their sip to a younger sibling or friend held tightly on their hip, not knowing if we would be able to give them another. We never had enough water to share, and I felt that what we could offer was like a cruel tease to those who managed to score a small drink. It was a heart-shattering daily ritual that I came to dread.

One of the older children helping us on the project was a South Sudanese teenager called Bosco. He and his much younger brother were living under some tarp near the school after losing their family while escaping across the border. He had no idea if they'd made it or if they would ever be reunited. But still he arrived earlier than necessary every day with the most upbeat enthusiasm imaginable. He helped to build large ladders from pieces of wood and rope so we could reach the highest points of the building, and he painted quicker and with more care than anyone else. He took so much pride in the work that he became something of an honorary project manager, doing his best to direct the hundreds of children running amok with oil-based paint and masking tape. He was a strapping, broad young man, despite his lack of access to good food, and he had managed to teach himself decent conversational English, despite his lack of access to proper education. His animated deep brown eyes staring out from above his protruding cheekbones broke my heart. I didn't understand where he found the energy to take on each day with such an abundance of eager joy.

And then there was my little Magdelena, another of the many unaccompanied children who miraculously managed to survive here day after day entirely alone. I still well up to this day when I think of her tiny, dirty bare feet and her big bright smile made even more prominent by her shaved head. She never spoke a word for the whole two weeks she attached herself to me, but we formed quite a bond. On maybe our second or third day on the project, surrounded by the ever-present sea of children that gathered at our feet as we worked, she pushed through the crowd in her tattered bright-red dress and clung to my ankle. This wasn't particularly unusual – children often came up to us and we were always more than happy to pick them up or have them sit with us for a while until they were ready to disappear back into the mass of faces. But Magdalena never left my side – every day she found me and walked with me as I painted or sat with me while I rested, but she only ever offered that big smile, albeit briefly, when I would pick her up and let her sit on my hip at the end of the day. To encourage that smile more often, we'd play skipping and draw pictures in the earth with pointed stones. Of course, any activity of this sort would attract every child within a wide radius to join in – the fun was always shared and never without the sounds of African drums somewhere in the background.

While I held Magdelena in my arms one afternoon, a local aid worker explained what the drums meant to this newly formed community and to most communities throughout Africa. The simple instrument played with the beat of bare hands was called a *djembe*, which is an abbreviation of a local saying that translates to 'everyone gather together in peace'. Immediately, the constant pulse of percussion that floated on the air mostly unnoticed became weighted in significance and defiant strength. I was just allowing myself to get carried away in a whimsical notion about it when, in the same breath, he began to tell me about reports of possible human trafficking taking place in the camp. The South Sudanese children were vulnerable refugees of war, mostly without guardians or caregivers. It was the most devastatingly perfect storm: a vast group of nameless and unprotected potential victims in a world of corruption. Magdalena's head was resting on my shoulder, and I felt the most gut-wrenching hopelessness and an overwhelming desire to take her away from this place so that she could be safe. When she caught my eye, the Shel Silverstein poem 'Listen to the Mustn'ts' was all that came to me in the moment to make us both feel better. I recited it over and over as we strolled back to the school, more as a comfort to myself in the bleakness of the situation, but Magdalena flashed me one of those big bright smiles and the tears rolled down my cheeks.

The last day of the project arrived too fast, but getting to stand back and admire the school in all its completed glory, painted rainbow bright inside and out, was the most wonderful moment – as was getting to see the children take some positive ownership of their building in this difficult place. We were told that the community had organised a show of local dance and percussion as a thank you to the project members, so we took our seats outside the school to watch the performance. Looking over the crowd in front of us, one thing was undeniable: the number of smiles. And when I thought about it, that had been the case every single day of the two weeks I'd spent among these people. I was baffled by their genuine delight. I was an indulged white Western woman with my arms around everything I could have ever wanted, yet still somehow standing on the precipice of a breakdown. I didn't have a clear grasp on what was happening inside of me then, but I was just starting to become physically sick with sadness. Part of me knew it like a whisper but not yet like the roar it would become, so this experience was an incredibly poignant one.

I still find it difficult to properly articulate what we were treated to that day, but I will do my best. The dancing and drumming began soft and rhythmical with about 20 performers in local costume and the rest of the crowd swaying and bounding in unison to the beat. The pace of the movement and the tempo of the drums built slowly, drawing members of the observing crowd into the centre performance like an unstoppable magnet to join the quickening stomp and rattle of tiny stones wrapped around the dancers' ankles. The drumbeat seemed to reflect the mood, which spiralled into a wild and frenzied yet somehow utterly coherent and delicate tribal ritual. The crowd performing the dance keep growing and growing until every single person in sight was a part of it. It was an otherworldly kaleidoscope of energy, passion, love and joy, a single heartbeat of movement circling a whirlpool of percussion. And even that description doesn't do it justice. I tried to capture it on film, but when I watched it back, it looked like nothing but chaos, void of all the magic and awe it had gifted. It was something that could only be experienced in person.

It seemed to me at the end of the spectacle that their happiness stemmed from the strength of their human connection and the tight bonds they had to their deeply rooted culture. No matter what and no matter where, they had this like an unwavering anchor, even in the face of devastation and little hope. I realised there was so much I didn't understand in that regard, that I was missing a fundamental building block of life, of happiness, of purpose, meaning or inner peace – something I couldn't yet put my finger on but that felt incredibly important to uncover. Were it not for this monumental trip, forged from the deepest fear of leaving this man's side for even a moment, I don't know if I would have had the strength of character or clarity of mind to leave Ireland and travel long-term when the time came. This visit reignited a passion that I had kept mostly dormant for a decade, a deep desire to explore the world, to visit places far away from the norm. My heart told me there was more to be gained for me out there than within the walls and books of any university.

Leaving the camp was a strange experience. Although I was looking forward to eating literally anything other than rice and beans, even that thought burdened me with guilt. It felt wrong that we just got to walk away to full bellies, warm showers and plump pillows. To safety, prospects and boundless opportunity. No one and nothing is guaranteed for any of us in this life, but it certainly felt like we took an unfair portion of the pie on a global scale. The children chased our car for as long as their small, thin legs would allow, and I watched tiny Magdalena disappear into the dust through the rear-view mirror. I couldn't look back, and I still think of her with the heaviest heart and every hope that she's thriving, because anything can be.

CHAPTER 9

the burnout

'When you know better, you do better'

MAYA ANGELOU

In 2010, a number of years prior to my rapidly approaching and seemingly unstoppable meltdown, my dad had hit his own personal roadblock – a challenging period that was likely produced, at least partially, by some of his repeated poor behaviours. But he is not unique in this regard. We are often the biggest unconscious orchestrators of our own suffering. Though our stories are all different, we all come with our share of shadows, shortcomings and blind spots. The extent to which we can become aware of these and then work to overcome them is also the extent to which we have any control over our happiness in this lifetime of mostly random events. Cue an extensive existential debate on free will? In my experience, opportunities for personal growth usually arise through situations that force us to face pain, loss or something else terribly uncomfortable. It comes at a cost, but the rewards are generally substantial. But life's also a renowned bitch – if we don't quite get the message the first time around, the lessons keep coming and they keep getting louder and more frequent. Perhaps my dad had been ignoring his shadow parts for some time because this particular life lesson nearly broke him completely.

At the time, we still had a poor and distant relationship. I knew he was struggling mostly because of the toll it was taking on my mother, who was kept awake most nights listening to him pacing the landing for hours on end, sick with worry. For a year or more he battled with this personal obstacle at the expense of his well-being, which finally began to display its underlying corrosion in an undeniable and dramatic shift in his general demeanour and appearance. In my eyes, he went from being a broad-chested, domineering figure of ultimate authority to a meek, nervous and almost hunched shadow of his former self. It was as if he was attempting to fill less space, to quietly disappear. His hands shook while he went about humdrum tasks in the kitchen and he looked distinctly more grey, weak and weathered. I almost couldn't align the two identities in my head – the man I knew my father to be and the man now standing before me were growing apart. But we rarely exchanged more than pleasantries and perhaps a brief life update, and I was uncomfortable at even the notion of sitting down to speak with him about anything remotely deeper than that.

I kept my distance and got most of my information about what was happening with him through my mam. I would never have turned to him for support and he would never turn to me. Which made it all the more unsettling when, one evening, I heard the timid rattle of his knuckles on my bedroom door. I was at home for some reason, my brother no longer lived at my parents' house and my mam was out, meaning I'd stay in my bedroom, a habit that came from years of fear of passing him in some common room of the house, which only ever resulted in skin-crawling awkwardness.

When I opened the door, my dad stood slumped in the hallway, his face pale as snow and his eyes sunk deep in his sockets. He was fumbling with the nails on his trembling index fingers before he looked up at me and said, 'I need you to take me to the doctor. I'm going to kill myself.'

At that time, my ability to quickly and effectively forget or avoid the things that hurt me most was a well-honed skill, and while this painful interaction was the beginning of some slow, necessary changes, I banished it and the events that followed it to the recesses of my mind almost immediately. I did not remember it whatsoever for many years after, and when it finally did resurface into my consciousness, I wasn't sure whether I had, in fact, made it up. I got the answer to that question only when I, too, reached the furthest depths of my own breakdown. As you will soon see, I am my father's daughter.

○ ○ ○

'I have the flu again and my voice is going.'

This is how my complaints would begin. Through the last half of 2016 and into 2017, I made more visits to my childhood GP's clinic than ever before, attempting to explain any one or more of the physical symptoms of burnout I was experiencing. Losing my voice was extremely inconvenient when I needed to host a breakfast radio show in the capital Monday to Friday, but the remedy frustrated me even more. 'Rest' wasn't something I had time for.

On another visit: 'I'm just so tired all the time – I'm not functioning properly and my head feels fuzzy. I'm having really uncomfortable digestive issues every day too, and I have this constant twitch that alternates between the top and bottom of my left eyelid.' This was another inconvenient set of symptoms when I worked most days after the breakfast show as a model. Significant gut distension and breakouts made bikini photo shoots even more stressful than realising you are probably already too old to be doing them. Plus trying to smize convincingly through the aggressive and persistent twitch in my eye became a weekly problem. I took adrenal support, strictly implemented the results of my food intolerance test and generously rubbed magnesium oil on my skin at 1 a.m. when I had to be up for work at 5 a.m. – it was supposed to help with the insomnia and thus cure the twitch, but clearly it wasn't working. In fact, none of the prescribed solutions to any problems I presented with ever worked because singly addressing the manifestations of a root cause is like putting Steri-Strips on a bullet wound.

So the visits continued to clock up as life whirled by and the complaints became more elaborate with time. 'When I breathe in it's like a sharp shooting pain in my chest, but if I force myself to inhale deeply enough through the pain, it feels like it pops and then the pressure in my chest eases. And remember that twitch in my eye I was telling you about? Can you get those in your heart too? Because I'm pretty sure I have one in my heart now – even when there's no pain I feel like it's beating funny.' On the basis of this description, my GP sent me for an ECG to rule out any abnormalities. During the wait for testing and results, I spent most of my idle time ruminating on my imminent death by heart attack. Then my GP called to tell me my heart was perfectly healthy. The heart pain didn't stop, but this did give me permission to move on to preoccupying myself with worry about having early onset Alzheimer's instead, which I now know was actually the confusing beginning stages of a chronic panic disorder. After the first incident I told my GP, 'I was walking a trail I've walked so many times with a friend I've known since childhood, and then suddenly neither of them was familiar any more. I forgot where I was and I think I forgot *who* I was. It was the most powerful feeling of disorientation, like I was leaving my body. In the moment, I felt so overwhelmed with fear that I thought I might faint or vomit, or both. Then after a couple of minutes I began to settle and the world started to realign, but I still felt this ripple of fear for hours, actually maybe days, after. Sometimes I felt like I didn't want to leave my bed because any sensory stimulation at all was completely overwhelming in the aftermath.' My GP asked if anything particularly strange had happened immediately after the incident, 'like a sudden releasing of the bowels'. And while I was still battling chronic digestive issues every day, thankfully on this occasion I hadn't shit myself in public, no. I think she was trying to rule out any significant neurological malfunction but, regardless, she sent me for an MRI scan on my brain to be absolutely sure. Again, the results came back that my brain was structurally perfectly healthy.

When I returned to her with my latest fixation, 'a hard lump the size of a tennis ball in my lower abdomen', after an examination she informed me that stress might be the root cause of my ever-growing list of ailments. This was the first time anyone had made that connection in relation to me. Needless to say, it went in one ear and out the other before she'd even finished the sentence. I thought it was some kind of formality she needed to spiel off before she got back to talking facts and reason. But she continued to tell me how I must make some 'lifestyle changes' in order to improve my health. Yoga and meditation were noted as two worthy places to start. I was baffled because I was so clearly physically sick. Where was the diagnosis and the foil-covered sleeve of pills to make it go away? I left her office promising myself I'd get a second opinion once I could find a window of time to commit to the issue, which was already dominating my days with diet alterations, tests and tablet scheduling. I was a highly productive person, 'too together to fall apart' as one of my colleagues had pointed out. My breaking point and some of the darkest days of my life were just around the corner I was hurtling towards, but I couldn't see it coming. I had never taken a minute to get to know myself, to think about where I'd come from or where I was going. I simply never,

ever thought I would struggle with my mental health. I never thought I would be the victim of a breakdown, so even in the midst of it, I was in complete denial about what was happening with me. It just did not register on my radar.

Over the coming months, after my erratic non-stop crying phase and overlapping with the trip to Uganda, I tried to maintain the schedule of my regular day-to-day life, showing up for work and other commitments and ticking off the to-do lists on my daily Google calendar while also trying to be a good friend, a good girlfriend – despite the volatility of my new relationship – and an all-round sane and decent person in society at large. There were a number of days during those months where I found myself so desperate for relief from the confusing symptoms of my over-active sympathetic nervous system that I would try to sit down and meditate or book into an overpriced drop-in yoga class. Meditating just did not work for me – it felt like nothing but utter boredom and time-wasting, and on some occasions it seemed to be an opportunity for my mind to amplify every negative thought brimming with worry and catastrophe or to showcase a running commentary of everything I had failed to do so far in my life. I found that to be an unsettling experience, one to be avoided at all costs.

Yoga annoyed me from the outset. All the classes had similar yet completely elusive names, so I never knew which to choose; before even arriving, I was resentful at having to pay €20 for the privilege; and the pseudo-spiritual glad rags and decoration on far too many people in the room really pushed me over the edge – and this was with 90 minutes to go. 'Remember to breathe' was my least favourite repetitive statement, especially when said in a patronisingly soothing tone while I was quivering from head to toe, dripping in sweat, simmering just a notch below explosive levels of anger and trying to hold some contorted position. 'I've been breathing my entire fucking life, Linda, you sap,' I would scream on repeat in my head. Even when I tried my best to focus on breathing as directed, unbeknown to me I was taking short, rapid breaths into the highest part of my chest and making myself hyperventilate. I never left a class feeling anything other than ripped off, exhausted and irate. I'll be honest, the intensity of my reaction to yoga did alarm me and could have been an indication that there was something a little off with me, but I just resigned myself to the fact that it wasn't for me. I wasn't of the spiritual persuasion and that's OK – it was nonsense anyway was my mindset.

Then one morning I simply woke up feeling unbearably different – like something had snapped and I was no longer myself. It felt like a strange combination of insufferable nerves and numbness. The panic attack I described in the opening pages of this book had happened the day before, reducing me to an almost vegetative state in the aftermath. Once I'd made it home to the safety of my couch, my roommate had fed me a mashed banana as I trembled the evening away, waiting for the shockwaves to pass. But after that panic attack there were no more breaks from the overspill of stress, which had allowed me to function as somewhat normal. My mouth was always dry, my breath always short and rapid, my body shook and twitched and my head felt constantly muddled, like I was grasping at the thinnest edge, dangling above a hopeless, all-consuming pit of panic below. Food stopped tasting like anything at all, good or bad, and I couldn't find joy in any of the things that had sparked it in me before. I felt mostly nothing, other than the constant nerves. I lost all motivation to do anything more than stay in bed – even showering became a once-weekly trouble and only for everyone else's benefit.

I was still managing to drag myself to my work commitments on most days, digging deep to find the bare minimum amount of confidence and composure necessary to get me through the shift. I had become completely disillusioned with the career I had worked so hard and so long to build. It no longer brought me any happiness or purpose, and every time I was forced to say our breakfast show's sponsorship tagline – 'McDonald's, making mornings tastier' – or smile for another picture endorsing some product I wouldn't dream of using myself, I felt like nothing more than a soulless, fake, glorified walking billboard. And I mean that literally, as my giant smiling face was actually on rotation on a large city centre billboard right outside my living-room window. I had never, and probably will never again, experienced anything quite like the dissonance of that unrecognisable version of me beaming into my home as I tried to find some reason or the courage to simply dress myself.

But it wouldn't stay like this for long – it couldn't. The feeling of disorientation I had described to my GP months earlier had permeated my day-to-day life as recurring panic attacks with a side order of constantly fluctuating disassociation, so whether I liked it or not, I would soon no longer be able to work. Like most people who experience a panic disorder over an extended period of time, I developed agoraphobia, which is essentially an intense fear of leaving your bed in case you are overcome with the humiliating symptoms of fear and panic anywhere other than alone between the safety of your sheets. Being forced to venture into the city centre every day was nothing short of an assault, when everything felt potentially overwhelming and threatening. I felt highly vigilant at all times, even though I resided mentally in the thickest brain fog. Noises, smells, moving objects and even the feeling and sound of someone's footsteps behind me became a trigger for panic. That was a particular complex of mine – I grew to despise people walking behind me to the point that I would have to stop and let them pass. I would sometimes even be angry and rude in doing so – 'Can you just go by me?' On top of that, I developed an obsessive fear of choking on my food, so the already grim task of trying to force feed myself a tasteless meal was made even more difficult by my brain refusing to let me swallow without panicking. Alone in my bed, preoccupied by YouTube, was the only place I felt any semblance of calm and normality.

Even at this point I still wasn't convinced I was suffering from a mental health issue, so I did finally make the time to get that second opinion. I took an arduous 15-minute walk from my apartment to a GP's clinic on Dame Street, and over a long consultation I told him everything that had happened until that point. I left his office with no place to hide from the fact any longer. Staring at a prescription for antidepressants and Xanax, the penny finally dropped and I felt so ashamed. I had betrayed myself into a million broken pieces. How many times had I bulldozed through the many warning signs, ranging from a whisper to a roar, and ignored my overburdened body trying to seize my fractured attention for even a moment and for my own benefit? I had spent so long defiantly searching for the solution outside of myself when all I'd needed was a single cell of self-awareness to clock the actual cause of the problem. I was devastated to have arrived at this point, but I also felt the slightest, briefest glimmer of determination. With the desperate confusion untangled and an answer in hand, I was going to solve this.

Over the following days I handed in my notice at work, found a psychotherapist I could meet weekly and reduced my life to absolute basics. I started to properly research meditation, yoga and other self-care activities instead of ignorantly denouncing their scientifically proven benefits. Through this I found yin yoga, a slow and restorative class where you hold poses for up to five minutes, and finally, instead of getting angry, I would cry, leaving the class with a short-lived but refreshing feeling of relief. I tried acupuncture, Chinese medicine and sensory deprivation tanks, anything that would allow me to activate a relaxation response for any length of time. I bought every book I could find on the mechanics of anxiety and depression so that I could understand what was happening inside my body on a structural and hormonal level. The more I knew, the less there was to fear. I learned cognitive behavioural therapy techniques for grounding myself and reducing that well-oiled spiral into panic, which had been conditioned over and over through the accumulation of stress.

When your body has become accustomed to being in a fight-or-flight state, whether it's a constant hum of anxiety or a full-blown descent into uncontrollable panic, it takes time, patience and a lot of self-love to unlearn this pattern of behaviour. Even when you can rationally understand what is happening and why, rewiring your neural circuitry is a long-term commitment. So during this time of steady and considered work, I still felt like I was making little progress and would often drag myself many steps back with the certainty that I would never find the person I used to be. I was so scared. Scared to get out of bed in the morning, scared to be in the smallest and safest of social settings and, most of all, scared that I would never find my old self again. She was gone and this was simply my new prevailing, dreadful mindset. The meetings with my psychotherapist ranged from a weekly lifeline to an obligation I would dread – sometimes our conversations would induce a panic attack and I would come to associate her room with fear. We hopped around locations every other week to help with this. The process was slow, frustrating and laboured, but through talking and talking and talking, I began to identify my predisposition to stress from childhood and how my anxiety would lock its talons around me using my greatest fear, born from watching my mother suffer: illness.

I also began to notice how I used varying degrees of dissociation, from completely blocking something out to simply shutting down when it came to handling situations or triggers I perceived as highly stressful, and that's when we got to my dad. He was now a very gentle and reserved man, and our relationship hadn't been an issue for many years. We spoke, but not in depth or too regularly, and we had never addressed that we used to be absolute enemies or why that had changed. I assumed it was just a part of growing up, and I was resigned to the fact that my relationship with my dad had little to no bearing on me.

So I talked and talked some more, running through the events of my childhood and adolescence, until I came to that day in my early twenties when he had knocked on my bedroom door. I told her the entire story and quickly followed it with, 'But I don't know if that actually happened or if I'm just making it up.' She probed a little by asking, 'Well, what happened when you took your dad to the doctor?' I told her I didn't know. I had no memory of the drive and perhaps a vague memory of my dad slouched beside me on a chair while I explained to his GP why he had asked me to bring him there. 'And what happened after?'

she continued. But this is where my memory completely stopped. I didn't know if I had stayed in the room with my dad or left. I didn't remember taking him home. I didn't know if he had been given any treatment or admitted to hospital and I didn't remember ever speaking to him about it again after it had happened ... if it even had. What she prompted me to do next resulted in the single most healing and necessary moment of my entire life to that point: 'So go ask him.'

It took me a couple of days to build up the courage to ask my dad to meet. He knew I wasn't doing well at the time but, similar to my reaction while he was struggling, he'd mostly kept his distance and probably got his updates on my wellbeing from my mam. On the drive from the city to my family home in Kildare I was sick with nerves, just to add to the regular dose of nervous energy that generally accompanied my day to day. My hands were so sweaty that I was genuinely concerned about holding the steering wheel safely and considered pulling in or, even better, turning around. When I arrived at the house my dad was peeling and dicing potatoes in the kitchen, occupying himself with the task to make this bizarre scheduled meet-up seem less strange. We exchanged some mindless chat before he allowed a silence to fall between us, his own way of allowing me some space to bring up whatever it was I needed to discuss with him.

The truth is I wasn't sick with nerves for myself or for what I might or might not gain from this conversation. I was sick with nerves for my dad. Regardless of everything we'd been through, I loved him unconditionally and I never wanted to hurt him. After everything he'd worked so hard to overcome, the fear of dragging him backwards in any way scared me so much. He had fought to become the man he was now and I didn't want to break his heart. And so I told him I was scared to say what I felt I needed to, scared to ask him some questions and, most of all, scared to hurt him. He replied, 'Dell, I'm your dad. Anything you need to tell me you can, and you never, ever need to be scared of hurting me.' So with his permission, I did.

Through floods of unstoppable tears and gasps for breath, I told him everything I could remember from my childhood. In a long and meandering babble I ran through every incident and every grievance, all the bottled-up hurt and confusion, while he continued to peel and dice potatoes. When he was sure I had aired every word, he looked to me with the trails of his own tears visible down past his neck and said the only thing I needed to hear. 'I don't remember everything you've said there, Dell, no. But all I need to do is ask myself was I capable of everything you've said at that time, and the answer is yes. I am so sorry, Dell, I am so, so sorry and I love you.' The long overdue relief of this small string of sentences was almost too much to bear. He also confirmed that my memory of the night he rattled on my bedroom door hadn't been a complete fabrication: it had happened. He had reached rock bottom and he was now a better man for it. Apparently we had never spoken about it after – I must have just brought him home and retreated to my room, unsure of how to handle the crushing concern for a man I loved but didn't like.

I'm so grateful for that day that I'm almost grateful for the breakdown itself, as it is surely the only thing that could have brought me to that moment. From that point on our relationship began to mend and rebuild in ways I could never have imagined. I couldn't be prouder of my dad or more inspired by the peace and authenticity he has found within himself. So many people never face who they really are, never make peace with their past or put in the work to change or make amends. My dad and I have, and in the weeks that followed that day, I found the strength in me that had been missing, another seed of determination to overcome the battle I was fighting. Most of the people who cared about me wanted me to start the course of medication I had been prescribed, to move home and be surrounded by family while I worked through my difficulties. But I kept coming back to the feelings I had experienced in Thailand all those years ago, and more recently in Uganda. I knew in my gut that the source of my aliveness and the route back to myself wasn't to be found curled up in my childhood bedroom. It was out there in the world where I would rediscover my passion, my capacity and my resilience. Everyone thought it was the most ridiculous and counter-intuitive idea: to book a one-way ticket to travel the world alone, at my most vulnerable. Everyone, that is, except my dad. As I said before, we are cut from the same cloth and he knew I could do it – in fact, I think he knew I had to do it.

Once the decision was made, I left within a week with a one-way ticket and nothing but a vague plan in place.

PART TWO

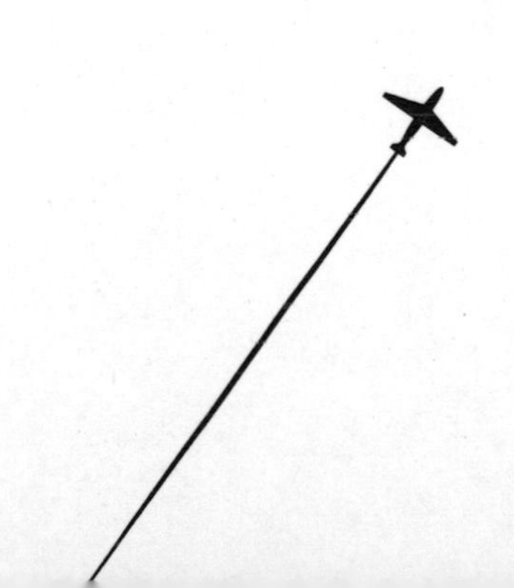

CHAPTER 10

burning man

'As to the methods, there may be a
million and then some, but principles
are few. The man who grasps principles
can successfully select his methods.
The man who tries methods, ignoring
principles, is sure to have trouble'

HARRINGTON EMERSON

The Burning Man Festival takes place over 10 days every September in Black Rock City in north-western Nevada. For 50 weeks a year this piece of land is nothing more than an arid lake basin until upwards of 70,000 like-minded people arrive to create a temporary community built on 10 simple shared principles. It is a concentrated bubble of the very best and most beautiful parts of the human spirit. Every one of your guards will drop here and you will be sincerely cheered for who you are beneath life's pressures and constraints. Compliments and genuine praise flow freely, small talk doesn't exist and you will experience a primal human connection that you didn't even know you were desperately missing. Wild and wonderful conversations, eye contact and genuine smiles with strangers and absolutely nothing filtered through phones or screens. It's truly mind-blowing how good this is for your soul. Learning how much emptiness resides in our everyday interactions and how I could change that is the most valuable gift I brought home…

Burning Man is a fervently respectful adult playground, the likes of which I'd challenge anyone to find the world over. You cannot and will not fail here. You will only grow in so many more ways than you ever thought you could…

I encourage you to put it on your bucket list. It will change your approach to life.

These are some extracts from a piece I wrote after attending my first burn, nearly a year to the day before my mental health was turned on its head, and reflecting on these words, the festival was clearly a welcome respite from the accumulation of stress in my life at the time. In hindsight, I think it did put the brakes on the steady dip of my brewing meltdown for a little while because it was an overwhelmingly enlightening experience, one I floated on for quite some time after – most likely because it was also the first time I tried psychedelic drugs. I had just turned 28 and up until that point the most experimental I'd ever got was a few drags on a bad joint. Weed just did not agree with me. It made me anxious and paranoid every time, inducing the kind of high I was willing to be over and putting me in a state that was a far cry from the slightly sedated, giggly sensation I'd anticipated. It had been hammered into me from a young age at home and in school that drugs are bad and if you take them you will die. So based on that information and the supporting handful of disappointing dabbles over my teenage years, I'd decided that drugs and me just did not match. I'd always been certain that I would be a member of the unlucky 1 per cent who tries ecstasy for the first time and ends up on the news as a tragic fatality. But the older I got and the more autonomy I gained over my thinking, the more bored I became with that story and the fear-mongering that always shrouded any further conversation on the topic. I was curious about the undeniable popularity of recreational drugs – it made sense to me that everyone must be doing them for a reason.

Not long before attending the festival that year, while reading a book called *Waking Up* written by neuroscientist Sam Harris, I came across a paragraph that read, 'These chemicals disclose layers of beauty that art is powerless to capture and for which the beauty of nature itself is a mere simulacrum. It is one thing to be awestruck by the sight of a giant redwood and amazed at the details of its history and underlying biology. It is quite another to spend an apparent eternity in egoless communion with it.' Sam Harris has dedicated most of his adult life to seeking an understanding of consciousness by altering his own state of consciousness and trying to experience this state in its purest form, without an attachment to the 'self'. He is so dedicated to this study that he spent two years meditating on a silent retreat, among many other extreme avenues of research. In this book he also wrote, 'I have two daughters who will one day take drugs. Of course, I will do everything in my power to see that they choose their drugs wisely, but a life lived entirely without drugs is neither foreseeable nor, I think, desirable … if they don't try a psychedelic at least once in their adult lives, I will wonder whether they had missed one of the most important rites of passage a human being can explore.' As a neuroscientist, his work is based on science rather than spirituality, and if this was the conclusion his extensive academic research had brought him to, it was grounds for me to start seriously questioning my conditioning.

Arriving at Burning Man, my mindset was primed and the setting was perfect. My first experience with psychedelic drugs was an astoundingly positive one, an explosive introduction to an inner world I'd never known. I spent 10 days in nirvana, at ease within the cosmos, flowing with the booming music and lunacy, surrounded by a constant dance of fire and lights. Every trip was more sublime than I could have ever imagined, unlocking boundless new levels of love, gratitude and joy I didn't know I was capable of, a freedom and escapism beyond anything I thought possible. Cut to a year later and I desperately wanted a repeat of the same, a return to the source of my greatest high to collect a quick bypass to a chemically induced expansive sense of place, purpose and meaning that would linger with the same rippling effects it had had the last time around. Somewhere in my own muddled logic, it made perfect sense for me to turn my back on prescription pills and run straight into the warm, open arms of some illegal class As. Of course, my mindset was entirely different on this occasion, filled mostly with fear, worry and a constant hum of uneasiness, and my experience this time around reflected that. Thankfully, I had the wherewithal to abstain from psychedelics, all too aware of their ability to hurtle you into a seemingly eternal state of pain, shame and torture indistinguishable from psychosis when the balance of your inner chemistry is awry. Instead, I ingested cocktails of synthetic dopamine-enhancing stimulants in search of the insightful beauty and happiness I had found there before. But of course it didn't happen like that. I couldn't tap into even a fraction of the wondrous, almost sacred realities I'd entered into in this same landscape just a year earlier. In fact, it was like the drugs didn't work at all. The highs were short-lived and messy, my serotonin levels so depleted on arrival that I was in a deficit after the first dab, but for 10 days straight I kept taking more and more.

The relief of being in a foreign place, away from every trigger and stressor, was almost exhilarating enough to fool me into thinking I felt some semblance of happiness over the first number of days. But then the comedown would hit me, and hard. So for the last half of the festival I was just doing my best to keep it at bay, knowing it would impose its full expression of sheer terror on me in the near future. Leaving the festival, I was exhausted and despondent, the little voice inside my head chattering relentlessly in catastrophic riddles, and as the hours ticked by I began literally writhing in my own skin. Over the following days, I fell into a depression so acute that for a split second while sitting alone in a car in San Francisco, I considered running out in front of traffic to make it all stop.

What the fuck was I doing? I'd left home determined to mend and heal, to do the travel thing where you find yourself amid the chaos of life. It had been less than three weeks and I'd already made everything so much worse, and of course I had, because I was still an idiot. Travel in and of itself will not help you figure anything out: all growth and insight is earned, and I was just not ready to put that work in yet. What travel did give me, whether I liked it or not, was time, an essential tool to start the process. And now, faced with nothing but time to consider the state I had got myself into, I booked a flight from San Francisco to Anchorage, Alaska, in search of a nature high instead of a chemical one. But that wouldn't be anywhere near the end of my self-medicating. For the next several months I'd turn to drugs as a source of relief over and over and over, until eventually I found a reason to stop.

But one of the most difficult things to overcome after leaving home was untangling my sense of self from that incredibly intense and utterly codependent year-long relationship I'd been in up until the day I'd walked onto the plane. I had always approached my romantic relationships with a guarded, withdrawn and almost masculine energy – until this one. For the first time, I thought I had allowed myself to crack open a window to a more gentle and feminine part of myself. In my utter obsession I had tried to lean into the relationship, to nurture it in a way I wished I had been capable of before, and still it hadn't worked. In fact, it had mostly contributed to the downward spiral of my mental health, yet I'd clung to it with all my might until the bitter end. It had broken my heart at a time when I was already broken, and only in my desperation to get well did I finally feel I had to forget it, for fear I would otherwise forget myself. In that headspace, trying to cultivate the emotional maturity necessary to forgive and move forward without holding onto anger, resentment, envy or any other horrible feeling that can linger from a break-up took months of reflection and self-talk, motivated through the many regressions by any ease in my sense of heartbreak. Alaska is where I would begin to accept that if I couldn't yet let it go, I at least had to let it be.

For seven days straight I hiked alone through some of the most treacherous trails I've ever encountered. It was autumn so the days were still just long enough to complete a 12-hour round trip through the dense mountain woodlands that surround the city in every direction. For about two weeks every year the country's thick covering of foliage turns bright burnt orange, yellow, gold and crimson, a truly impressive autumnal display that my visit overlapped with, and one that I would later learn gives the hiking trails a deceptively welcoming appearance. On one particularly hairy excursion, I left my rental car in the vast emptiness of a car park located somewhere two hours north of Anchorage, signed the ranger's log book left in a wooden box at the entrance to the trail so that they could identify me as a missing person if never returned to this spot and set off.

Alaskans really don't care for trail markings, paths or even defined openings in the thick forest landscape. If you choose to hike here you can expect to traverse multiple fast-flowing rivers up to your waist, navigate a path across a waterfall right along the edge of the drop where the flow is at its most rapid and simply figure it out when you keep sliding down some mucky slope that seems insurmountable. It is brutal and intimidating, pure rugged wilderness. On top of that, you have to shout '*Hey bear*' every couple of minutes to make sure you don't startle a native brown or black bear going about its business in the woods.

Food supplies sealed in a tin to conceal any attractive odour and bear mace primed and ready to dispense in my trembling hand, I walked to the summit without seeing another soul for six hours straight. A lot really does go through your mind in that length of time while alone in the middle of absolute nowhere, juggling severe anxiety and chemically induced depression, making sense of your heartache and the imminent threat of death by bear mauling. I quickly learned how to regulate the stream of thought predicting my demise, and once that bubbling, incessant fear peaked and broke, I discovered the most incredible sense of freedom on the other side. There is something truly indescribable about being so alone that not one person on this planet knows your whereabouts and maybe never would if anything were to go wrong. I highly recommend experiencing it at least once – as wild as it sounds, it's definitely character-building. Towards the end of the laboured ascent, when I finally broke through the thick canopy of tree cover and walked along the bare ridge of the mountaintop above the clouds, surrounded on all sides by even higher peaks carved by glaciers and out of which hundreds of long waterfalls seemed to spill, I felt like a fearless adventurer who could overcome anything life threw at me. It was magical. I sat for 30 minutes at the edge of a trickling stream, moved to tears by the serenity. Six hours of grappling with my mind's limitations was worth it for that moment of peace and the expansion of my understanding of my capacity.

Back in the safety of my hostel that night, still riding the high of my invigorating hike, I took to Instagram to share a selfie I'd taken at the summit of the trail with a long and meandering caption that included this extract:

Travelling alone forces you to push the limits of what you think you're capable of. It forces you to re-evaluate your inner strength and self-belief. You have no choice but to overcome fears, both big and small, every day. Otherwise you would surely succumb to the solitude, the loneliness or boredom enough to send you home. Already I'm beginning to discover a fierce little warrior inside of me ... and I fucking love her. The discomfort of every change and challenge is so necessary in figuring out what I'm really made of. Courage, integrity and compassion, the three traits I am currently most proud of.

What a load of bullshit social media is. In reality, I'd been gone less than a month and figured out nothing more definitive than a fear of being sober. I'd had a handful of good hours that day, a nature high perhaps, and I'd deemed that enough reason to project some fantasy version of myself online, an uplifting, independent woman. I didn't mean any harm, of course, and I believed every word as I wrote it. I also wasn't one for airing my dirty laundry or hardships on the internet but regarded sharing the good as always acceptable. I've come to realise that this is probably just as harmful to myself and to others in its own inauthentic way as a heavily curated post that bears little resemblance to reality. If you were to scroll through my very active Instagram feed over the months in which I was falling apart, you wouldn't have assumed anything was amiss – in fact, everything looked just rosy. I was all smiles managing a heavy rotation of work, travelling on occasion, attending weddings and events or flogging whatever piece of PrettyLittleThing clothing would help pay the bills that month. I have never cared enough about my social media accounts to use a uniform filter for a considered aesthetic or to curate a look and feel for my online persona, yet through many, many years of mindless, repetitive daily scrolling and uploading, I had still become unconsciously adept at managing this second version of myself – and her life looked great. How bizarre to have two versions of yourself running parallel in your head, whether you're aware of it or not.

After seven isolated and thought-filled days in Alaska, I'd had more than my fill of my own company. I was also feeling more upbeat after being mostly alone in the woods, so I decided it was time to move onwards to nearby Vancouver to visit a school friend who was living there. The night I arrived I got high as a kite on MDMA and hopped three dangerously tall fences to attend a Bonobo concert in a city park – the Canadian security, who were accustomed to the behaviour of the very civil, sober and lawful local population, were no match for my brazen Irish ingenuity. I was having a ball, and I noticed the comedown wasn't as bad when you spaced out your highs as opposed to going hard at it for 10 days straight – who knew? Over the month or so that followed I continued to distract myself with new places, new people and every lovely numbing drug I could get my hands on – all while maintaining the persona of perfect sobriety and contentment online, by the way.

From Vancouver I headed south through Seattle and down along the west coast of California until I hit Los Angeles to stay with another friend from home. I've always loved LA, but anyone who's been there can confirm it is the perfect vortex of distraction and anonymity, a superficial city of endless opportunity, a place where nobody demands a shred of authenticity beyond whatever beautiful, together shell you choose to present – and there's a nice stretch of beach. Ideal. On the evenings we'd go out for dinner, I would require a bottle of wine to cope with the sensory demands of a busy restaurant, but to consider a further outing into the night, the support of some personality-propping drugs was needed without exception. I was still dealing with a constant simmer of daily anxiety and these substances were the only thing that allowed me to function in social settings without having to curl up into a ball in the corner. On my last night in the city we really went for it. I had to be up in the early hours of the morning to board an expensive last-minute flight I'd booked to Costa Rica, but that didn't stop me from swallowing a small parcel of MDMA and dissolving another few rocks in my vodka and cranberry for good measure. It was just an added bonus when I befriended the very generous owner of a few grams of cocaine. The night passed by quickly and all that remains from it now is some vague flashing memories of me, a girl from Kildare, twerking definitely very well in an LA drag club and then sitting on my friend's balcony as the sun came up, screaming '*Do you know how much I love you?*' down at the phone at my brother and a selection of others I'd decided to annoy during their workday thanks to the time difference. In the middle of one such forced conversation, it suddenly dawned on me that I'd a flight to catch, and as I began to wrap it up with a couple more declarations of love and an explanation that I had to get to the airport, my wise old friend on the other end of the phone informed me that I was 'so high you'll 100 per cent get arrested if you go to the airport right now'. He also demanded I give the phone to the friend I was staying with and proceeded to make him promise that he would not let me leave for the airport in the condition I was in.

Now I've never been arrested for the use of narcotics in the United States, but I'm sure it would be a costly and incredibly distressing experience, so I'm very grateful to have been stopped in my delirious tracks that morning. I couldn't even regret missing that overpriced flight when the alternative was calling my family for a six-figure bail. But waking up on my friend's couch later that day as night began to creep across the skyline outside his window, I was beyond disoriented. It took a few minutes for the previous night and the decisions I'd made as a result of it to reassemble in my head, and when they did I was awash with self-loathing and an uncontrollable case of the shakes. I tried to sleep it off and promised myself I would make amends and get back on track the following morning. But I'd slept for the entire day, so of course sleep would elude me for the night. Instead, I spent it mostly twitching myself in and out of a twilight state, sweating profusely and trying to decide if I was actually having a heart attack or not. I think it's safe to say that at this point I'd probably lost sight of why I'd started to experiment with drugs in the first place – there was no profound beauty to be found here, no insightful exploration of an inner world. I'd left home over two months ago and, outside of my week-long stay in Alaska, I hadn't spent any time alone or outside of my comfort zone. I'd been safely hopping from friend to friend and high to high. The thoughts came loud and fast. Maybe I was supposed to miss that flight to Costa Rica. Maybe I couldn't do it. Maybe the world really was a scary and dangerous place, and maybe I would just stay in LA with my friend and all the comforts of home a little longer.

In fact, maybe I should book a flight home.

In the dark of a fear-filled night, as soon as that thought broke through into conscious consideration, I rescheduled my flight from LA to Costa Rica for the next possible departure on a backpacker's budget and told myself this was the real beginning.

I could do this. I *would* do this.

CHAPTER 11

the bungee jump in costa rica

'Do it trembling if you must, but do it'

EMMET FOX

You may have heard that simple Buddhist proverb 'the obstacle is the path', or maybe the Benjamin Franklin quote, 'Those things that hurt, instruct.'

While plodding along in my regular life I'd never needed to take much heed of these nuggets of wisdom, because for me, just like for everyone else, as long as our habitual ways of being in the world are working for us, whether they're helpful to us or not, we have no reason to pay attention, no reason to change, no reason to look inward. We are enslaved to our conditioning, ruled by our personal histories, survival strategies, distortions, socially constructed personas and habits. The day these internal maps reach their sell by date is always around the time we find ourselves up against a wall, experiencing a personal trauma or a high degree of suffering, a situation in which the ways that we are in the world no longer work.

This hurt, pain, dissatisfaction or discomfort is a necessary prerequisite to change: it forces us out of complacency and invites us to move towards self-transformation – if, and only if, we can first transcend the anxiety that comes hand in hand with leaving the comfort of the familiar to journey to a new reality, entirely unsure of what we'll find along the way, a sort of personal pilgrimage. Everyone will experience suffering – there is certainly no lack of it – so why aren't all of us magically transformed as a result? Because it's fucking terrifying, that's why. Leaving behind what we know about how the world works and how we work in it is destabilising and nothing short of harrowing. It's easier to fall back into our old patterns to avoid this scary, disorienting space between the old and the new, so that's almost always what we do. We cling to what is familiar because even if it hurts us over and over, it feels safe.

Except when we can't go back.

When we cannot un-know what we now know. When we willingly or unwillingly recognise and accept that what has worked for us before can simply no longer work. This is a key realisation on the path to self-discovery and to overcoming painful cycles, one I had purely thanks to intuition and without any of this clarity on the night I booked that second flight to Costa Rica. All I knew then was that, time and again, I'd observed in my own life that the greater the inner resistance I'd experienced around any given task or change, big or small, the more likely it was that that exact thing would end up being a direct path to some level of personal evolution. Only by continuously putting one shaky foot in front of the other did I begin to overcome that resistance and learn to use my own reasoning and willpower to confront even my most strongly held self-limiting beliefs head on, eventually allowing me to create a new expanded, even liberated, identity.

o o o

'Pura Vida' is the national motto of Costa Rica. It means 'simple life' and that's exactly what I was chasing when I arrived alone and hung-over to that beautiful place. By now my affinity for nature is probably very clear, so the fact that Costa Rica is one of the most biodiverse and environmentally vigilant countries on earth played a large part in my spontaneous decision to fly there. However, re-exposure to dengue fever had remained a simmering background worry for me among the noise of everything else, preventing me from really getting started with this travel thing, and arriving in Costa Rica, I knew I was stepping into that risk. But it was one I knew I had to face, one that felt worthwhile, necessary even. And I had high hopes that in taking the risk, Costa Rica would become my true starting point on this journey to figuring myself out. On top of that, there would be no comfortable distractions to turn to – I knew no one there and had no set plans.

At the airport I rented a dangerously old but appropriately cheap hatchback. It was monsoon season, business was slow and the price kept dropping the longer I agreed to rent it for. After a dance of feigned disinterest, nods to the other options available and writing off every hidden charge possible, I left the arrivals hall with the keys to my rattling, unpredictable chariot and the endless possibilities of the open road. Costa Rica would be my home for the next month. I picked up a local SIM card, a windscreen suction phone holder and a big bag of spiky red-skinned fruit called rambutan from a street vendor before offloading my backpack into the backseat and deciding on a whim to head for the Caribbean coast. With the sun setting in my rear-view mirror while driving Costa Rica's winding, bumpy roads through rolling hills of dense rainforest and intermittent blasts of static and flamenco guitar playing from my radio as my only company, I felt the small seeds of that aliveness I'd gone in search of. And, my god, was it good to feel a stir of positive emotion bubble inside me, naturally occurring, without the need for any synthetic catalyst. I'd never been afraid of travel – I'd been petrified that it wouldn't offer the sort of salvation I was looking for. But in those first steps I found that whisper of surrender, a belief that, in fact, the answers were inside me if I could just keep going.

My first stop was the small Rastafarian hub of Puerto Viejo de Talamanca. Seashell-trinket touts, fruit stalls, surf shacks, rustic bamboo bars and stand after stand of Bob Marley T-shirts lined every sandy street running back into the jungle from the ocean road. The smell of hash and guaro, a local drink made from sugar-cane, was a constant swirl in the air. After a night of research sitting beneath the moon, lit by the string of lights strewn across the palm trees that lined the shore outside my stuffy hostel dorm room, it occurred to me that of the 8 billion people on this earth, only 12 of us were lucky enough to be doing next to nothing midweek in this ramshackle jungle home on the outskirts of this little town in Costa Rica. I was doing something right, even if by society's standards I was kind of a train wreck, much too old to be single, without a property, a career, any possessions or prospects to speak of. But I wouldn't have time to think about that because, thanks to that night-time research, my itinerary was now jam-packed.

The next morning I woke with a stiff neck to the sound of a stranger's unsettling snores while hanging dangerously close to the edge of my very slim top bunk, ready to kick-start my over-zealous sightseeing plan with a trip to a local sloth sanctuary, which was home to upwards of 120 of Costa Rica's most lovable, sleepy creatures, rescued, rehabilitated and hopefully released back into the wild. I genuinely considered packing it all in right there and then to volunteer my assistance indefinitely. But that would mean staying in one place and perhaps sitting still with myself as a result. Instead, I filled every day from start to finish. I took surf lessons on Playa Cocles, went snorkelling through the coral reefs just off the coast at Grape Point, visited the people of the Bribri indigenous communities to learn about their customs, traditions and ways of living. I spent days beach-hopping and even went on a fishing trip (I hate fishing). I visited a jaguar rescue centre and a project working to re-establish macaw parrots in the region. And once I had absolutely everything ticked off the to-do list, I was on the road again.

My next stop was the lusciously green, lazy town of Dominical on the opposite side of the country. It had taken me two mostly unbroken days to travel the distance, the lucky recipient of a non-stop 'Costa Rican massage' in the process – the locals' description of the sensation of driving on the country's mostly unpaved roads. Exhausted on arrival, I booked myself straight in for a sunset tandem paraglide. It is arguably one of the most beautiful places in the world to sprint off the side of a hill to fly like a bird – twisting and spinning through the sky over the Dominical rainforest and coastline, eye to eye with hawks, spotting waterfalls hidden in the mountains below my dangling feet. Every day an abundance of novelty was on offer and I began to find great comfort in the constant change and my own capacity to handle it. I would spend long days hiking through Hacienda Barú, trying to spot all 330 species of wildlife that call this refuge home, or trekking deep into the remote tropical rainforest surrounding the town. On one such trek I slept in a cave lit by candlelight and hidden behind the 85-foot drop of the Diamante Falls. Falling asleep to the sound of rushing water was pure serenity, and I credited these experiences for the subsiding of my anxiety, day after day, without considering that I had removed every element of real-life stress, which may have also been helping.

From Dominical I travelled north to Manuel Antonio National Park, an area alive with the calls of birds and monkeys, thick rainforest vegetation and long beautiful beaches. Every day I had a new activity scheduled: white-water rafting, an ATV tour, kayaking and jet skiing. One evening I got home a little earlier than expected and took a last-minute Segway tour to fill the time slot. As is probably becoming clear, in travel, much like at home, I was doing a variation of what I'd always done: keeping busy.

With all my options exhausted in Manuel Antonio, I put my car on a ferry in the grubby port town of Punta Arenas to make the short gulf crossing to the tip of the Nicoya Peninsula. Here I stationed myself in an almost empty hostel, also functioning as a non-profit Spanish school, in the tiny endearing beach town of Montezuma and kept up the same enthusiasm for activities as I had in every stop prior. Montezuma Beach is where the olive ridley turtles come to nest. So every afternoon at four, I'd go to the ocean front along with the volunteers helping with a local turtle conservation project to help release a batch of hatchlings into the waves of their new home. On my way home one such evening, my head stuck in my phone booking a snorkelling and island-hopping excursion for the following morning, I walked into the makeshift stand of a topless older man with long, scruffy dreads selling handcrafted jewellery and bundles of herbs. Startled, I apologised, picked up anything that had fallen and started to head on my way until he called after me, 'You have a nervous energy that doesn't belong in you.'

The story to come might sound clichéd, but among the mostly mindless and increasingly fun days I spent roaming the globe with no real rhyme or reason, I occasionally experienced moments or interactions that resulted in some self-enquiry, which, over time, pieced together to form coherent answers. Walking into this man's table was one such interaction. I can't remember his name, but he had a gentle face and skin like old leather, decorated with many hand-poked tattoos and excesses of dangling crystals and jewellery. His linen harem pants hung low on his thin hips. He looked like every bohemian runaway I'd ever met on the side of any street in any remote beach town that allowed them to live a slow, steady, off-the-grid life. Sitting beside him, he smelled of musty jojoba oil, tobacco and sage, his gaze so unrelenting it made me slightly uncomfortable. But travelling alone, I'd come to live for these meetings of two souls whose paths never should have crossed, a brief entry into someone else's world.

He was a travelling shaman from Peru, an energy healer and a devotee to the powers of medicinal herbs. We spoke for hours about our lives, where we came from and what had brought us both to this unassuming place. He asked if he could tell me why he'd called after me and I told him he could. 'You are a very kind and soft person, much too full with fear and anger. You will never give to the world that which you are here to until you can forgive and get back in touch with your true essence. You have come far already because you are strong, resilient and independent, but inside you are afraid, much too afraid. You must overcome this. Beyond your fear you'll find your peace and your purpose.'

I loved his altruistic musings on my inner world, the flowery poetry of his words and the feeling that I was actually Julia Roberts in *Eat, Pray, Love* at that very moment. His meanderings about my gateway to contentment didn't carry much weight with me there and then, but his company and conversation were more appealing than spending the evening trying to connect to the shit Wi-Fi in my very cheap hostel dorm so that I could disappear down a YouTube rabbit hole.

His tales of medicinal herbs and their many uses intrigued me, as did his hopes that his work would add to the knowledge passed down to him by generations before. I've always felt a great humility in nature, an understanding that the complex yet delicate riddles of its perfect synergy hold an intelligence far beyond our grasp, maybe since I was a child concocting imagined elixirs from the leaves and flowers in our back garden.

He told me about the tribal ritual of *rapé*, pronounced *ha-pay*. Originating from the indigenous tribes of the Amazon basin, it is a carefully prepared blend of powdered medicinal herbs with profound healing effects, an ancient science, a sacred shamanic rite of passage that eventually travelled as tobacco-based snuff to the elites of European aristocracy as far back as the 1500s. Of course, the thought crossed my mind that this was the stupidest thing I'd ever considered doing, that it was quite worryingly called 'rape' with just a little hat on the e and that this man could be a liar and a lunatic, out to rob, hurt or even kill me – but how often was I going to find myself in a faraway jungle clearing on the furthest edge of a peninsula in Costa Rica, sitting on a rustic street with a wandering new-age Peruvian shaman? Trusting my gut, I told myself *amor fati*, a love of fate, as he forcefully blew the powdered mixture up my nose through a specially made bamboo straw. Instantly the billions of intricate neural networks – or arguably fewer, given the riskiness of this decision – that make up the complex executive functioning of my prefrontal cortex lit up with the unsettling strength of a lightning bolt only to subside, like fog parting in the wind, revealing the deepest sense of calm and clarity.

What ensued probably sounds like a predictable extension of this tale of hippy absurdity, but to me it felt, at least temporarily, life-altering. He was chanting when I opened my eyes again. I'm not sure how long I'd had them closed or how long it had taken for me to transition from the electric introduction to the stillness of the aftermath. But I didn't feel high like I'd expected – I felt grounded, peaceful and clear, with an overwhelming urge to go watch the sunset. I told him so, thanked him for everything, stood up and strode purposefully down the street as he called after me again, 'Don't be afraid.' I was a woman on a mission as I hopped on the back of a local driver's motorbike with the instruction to take me to the neighbouring village of Santa Teresa.

I had driven to Santa Teresa from Montezuma a number of times already and had fallen in full teenage-like love with everything about it. It was my favourite stretch of paradise in all of Costa Rica, a small hodge-podge coastal community of surfers, artists and yogis hidden at the end of the most awful attempt at a road, offering soul-serving sunset views every evening without exception.

Alighting from the bike, I could feel the pure vitality of everything that I generally overlooked. Floating along with the balmy breeze, I noticed the crunching sound and sensation of leaves, sticks and sand beneath my bare feet and the light taste of sea salt on my tongue. The pathway to the ocean was lined with palm trees that seemed to be swaying in perfect unison, beckoning me forward with the warmest welcome, while beams of golden sunlight danced through the veins of their transparent leaves to highlight small gatherings of flies swirling and spiralling in space. Santa Teresa Beach has to be one of the most exemplary showcases of untouched natural beauty on the planet, and in just stepping over the threshold of the pathway's end and on to its impressive expanse, my eyes filled with tears. Sitting cross-legged on the warm sand, gaze locked on the vivid spectrum of sunset shades before me, I felt the most peaceful sense of belonging, an encompassing sensation of home. From this rare moment of balance and quiet in my mind, a mantra came to me as if I'd been reciting these lines my whole life:

I am grateful.
I am pure love.
Love and light surround me.
Abundance unfolds before me.
Bliss is my default state.

I said it over and over until the sun disappeared behind the horizon and the bright pink sky began to turn a deep, dusky purple. The surfers were starting to return to dry land as the light of day gave way to the cover of night, and I got chatting to one of them as he dropped his board on a fallen log beside me, a curly-haired Mauritian named Yoni, which is also the Sanskrit word for the female genitals or, as he repositioned it, 'the source of all life'.

After a lengthy discussion about his unusual name to break the ice, he asked if I had any plans for that night, and for once I didn't. 'Good' was his simple reply. I watched him dig a small pit in the sand and build a brilliant, bright fire from dried sticks and dead vegetation he collected along the edge of the beach where it met the jungle. 'Keep warm, I'll be right back,' he said. From the hostel nearby, he returned with two blankets, a pizza and a bucket of beers. 'You have one hour to tell me all about yourself and why you're sitting on this beach alone, and then we're going on an adventure.' In my heightened state, that hour-long chat was one of the deepest human connections I'd experienced with a stranger. The flow of conversation was easy and familiar, its contents revealing and vulnerable.

I would generally still refrain from going on a night-time outing to an undisclosed location with a man I'd met an hour previously, but in the spirit of being unafraid and trusting in the magic of how this day was unfolding, I hopped aboard a van headed to 'somewhere spectacular'. Just under two hours later, thanks to Costa Rica's many impassable roads, we arrived at the opposite coast of this small peninsula, to a point called Bahia Beach. 'On the entire planet there are five locations where you can see truly vibrant bioluminescent water – this spot right here is number one,' Yoni informed me as he pushed me away from the shore in my one-man kayak and threw me an oar. 'Follow me, I know the best areas.'

I wasn't entirely sure what to expect, but as I drifted along behind him I began to notice the water sparkle a bright highlighter blue every time my oar moved through it. It was the most concentrated, dazzling display of nature's brilliance I have ever witnessed first hand. The sea glittered brighter than the night sky above us, but just in case that wasn't enough, a lightning storm started. Every few minutes the black night was lit ablaze and then the thunder boomed frighteningly loud. In the interludes of darkness, shining, zipping fireflies filled the gaps between the stars and bioluminescent water danced beneath my oar and my hands. It was simultaneously the most exciting and most serene moment and I was so utterly present, observing from a single, steady stream of consciousness rather than battling a rampant surge of noisy thoughts mostly unrelated to the moment I was living in.

This wonderful, unexpected day, these two serendipitous encounters and their resulting flow of experience had given me a powerful glimpse into the kind of state my mind could reside in. It was an entirely new way of being in the world if I could just learn how to get there regularly.

Travel quickly makes you comfortable with goodbyes, an almost daily occurrence as you move from place to place, meeting and losing people along the way, but parting from Yoni that night felt heavier than usual, as did deciding it was time to leave Montezuma. In the 24 hours after that magical display of thunder and lightning came widespread news of a red weather warning across the country. I heard it on the bulletin playing from my struggling car radio as I drove north with plans to explore the remote Guanacaste province of the north-west. Given that every road in Costa Rica is in dire need of attention, as were the treads of my four tires, the increasing intensity of the rainfall brought a correlated increase in the likelihood of my death by road accident. I called it a day when my back wheels slid on loose gravel, throwing me into a skid that stopped just shy of a large unguarded drop onto the rainforest canopy below. Utilising my painfully slow mobile data under the deafening sound of the rain on my car roof, a mere two hours later I found a place to stay for the night just a couple of minutes from where I'd nearly spun off-road – an eco-lodge and yoga retreat high on a hill overlooking the Cañafistula Valley.

Finding this place turned out to be a bit of luck because, within hours of settling in to my tiny wooden chalet, electricity and running water went off across the country and stayed off for the next four days. Everything went into lockdown as the storm battered the country's already impaired infrastructure, causing devastating flooding that killed 11 people and displaced half a million more by destroying their homes. Staying at an elevation meant myself, the two lodge owners, two chefs, two yoga teachers, a masseuse and eight American girls on a unfortunately timed yoga holiday were at the mercy of the severe winds but mostly safe from the flooding, and without any electricity we had no idea how bad things were below us. The government declared a national state of emergency, enlisting aid from global humanitarian organisations, while we were obliviously kept fed, warm, dry, safe and massaged throughout the whole ordeal. With fallen trees blocking the only road in or out and torrential rain bucketing from the heavens, I was made an honorary member of the retreat and we had little else to do but spend our days in long hatha flows, slow restorative classes or guided meditation. Forced to sit quietly without distraction, when my mind wasn't aimlessly wandering or worrying about hypotheticals, I thought a lot about that feeling of pure presence I'd had just a couple of days earlier. I tried hard to meditate it back into lasting existence, but of course failed miserably and grew frustrated instead.

Denied access to everlasting inner bliss on these initial attempts, I found myself giving more thought to the words of my wise Peruvian shaman. He'd said I was full of fear and anger, and having secured the smallest degree of distance from the grasp of daily anxiety, I had to agree that my predominant emotion for the longest time had been pure fear. The anger part I couldn't quite identify with because I'd been managing to partake in daily yoga classes just fine without turning into the Hulk even once. But I recognised that I had been living in a state of disorientation, detachment and general unease combined with an ever-present stream of hazy, despairing thoughts up until recently. I had been so scared every waking minute of the day and sometimes through sleepless nights too. I had stopped trusting myself and I had stopped trusting my body. I had become a bystander to my erratic emotions, waiting to spiral out of control, perhaps tipped over the edge by something as simple as footsteps walking too close nearby. The voice in my head hadn't spoken kind, empowering words in a long time – instead, it often told me I was weak and unworthy, sometimes destined for failure.

Sitting in a yoga shala on a hill, submerged in the sound of wind and rain and the hum of my own thoughts, ruminating on my relationship with fear, I realised I had started to confront it just by getting there. In leaving home and committing to this journey, and in stepping up as best I could in every scenario, my self-esteem was rising and I was regaining trust in myself. I was uncovering resilience and capacity I didn't know I had. Our worlds are shaped by the stories we tell ourselves, and I did not want my one shot at this life to be limited by my unchecked negative emotions, so I decided I would start pushing the confines of my fear. I would use this time to see what I was made of, to start actively conquering things I never thought I could. There was nothing to lose in doing so, as I could always retreat to my comfortable baseline of experience, but there was potentially so much to gain.

With the passing of the storm came our reconnection to civilisation and a broader understanding of the impact of the previous days. It was a stark reminder of how everything can change in an instant, and I felt genuine gratitude for having weathered the experience with such ease. Further stirred on by my short stint of reflection, I'd already decided on my next stop: the cloud forest town of Monteverde, famous for its array of extreme sports, most notably ziplining and bungee jumping.

The locals in Monteverde claim to have invented ziplining as a way to deliver lunch to its workers, so it is now appropriately home to Latin America's highest and longest line, 2 kilometres of pure terror, way too far above the earth, which you ride Superman-style. I'd read about it and had no intention of doing it until I decided I was ready to get uncomfortable in the name of growth. With surprising ease, I worked my way through all 10 of the course's incrementally terrifying jungle cables, only hesitating momentarily on the last one, which involved being pushed face down off the edge of a platform that dropped a sickening 150 metres or so to the ground below, and still I'd managed to open my eyes to enjoy the views while the sheer force of the wind tried to pull the skin off my face. I was delighted with myself and ready to head for a celebratory beer with the tour group until I was informed of the day's bonus activity: a bungee jump that swings over the jungle canopy, invitingly named the Mega Tarzan. I felt physically sick, the palms of my hands and the soles of my feet began to sweat at just the thought and my breath caught high in my chest. I'd decided to investigate my reaction to fear, and I was getting an undeniable insight right then. A bungee jump rated so highly on the list of things I'd never even consider doing that it hadn't been on my radar. Surely I was allowed to start small with this fear thing, ease into it?

I sat on a bench a good distance away from the beginning of the thin, bouncing suspended walkway that led to the jumping point and watched person after person from my tour group disappear off the end with a step and a high-pitched scream. A handful decided to call it a day, skip the jump and head back to the safety of the café at the park entrance. Knowing I had that option made it worse. The knot in my stomach grew with every passing minute as I racked my brain trying to find the courage or resolve to take that first step.

'You're up.' I was the last of the group and I knew it was now or never. I stood with shaking legs, sweating everywhere, and told myself to just walk to the start of the suspended walkway. Standing at the point where it left solid ground to float above the earth, I noticed it was made with grates that only slightly obstructed the view to the drop below. Fear is an interesting thing; I had just spent a day enjoying the adrenaline of heights and I hadn't even flinched at the idea of a tandem paraglide back in Dominical, yet here I was, petrified to the point of paralysis, and all it came down to was my own perception. It turns out that the story you tell yourself about something will have a great impact on how that thing affects you. I tried to rationalise the fear and walk, heart thumping and face forward, to the end of the platform, resistance like I'd never felt before building with every forced step. Trembling, mute, gaze locked directly in front of me, I was fitted with a harness and told to step off immediately when they opened the gate on a count of three. The bungee cord pulled me forward and into the drop disturbingly against my will. 'One … two …'

'Stop! No!' I couldn't do it. I could barely move at all, frozen stiff on the spot. My survival instinct had hijacked every cell of my body – the fear was just too much. I'd failed, but I could live with it: nothing in the world was worth feeling like this. Guided back off the suspension pathway by two concerned employees, I fell to my knees and vomited.

In the car on the way back to town, battling new levels of unexpended adrenaline rushing through my veins, I was so angry with myself.

I knew logically that nothing would go wrong on that bungee jump – what was I so afraid of? Why had I not acquired enough understanding or control of my emotions to bypass even the most powerful resistance when all that was on the other side was a single step into a few seconds of harnessed free-fall? I tried to shake the awful disappointment all through the afternoon and into the evening, but it only got worse as I recalled all the times I'd let my fear become an irrationally limiting thing that seemed to possess me rather than inform me. In a moment of utter frustration I called the tour company. 'If I come back right now, can I pay to do just the Mega Tarzan?' I asked. The manager remembered me from earlier, the girl who'd vomited at the entrance to his bungee jump, and replied, 'If you come back right now, I will personally walk you to the end of the platform and make sure you jump, free of charge.' That familiar surge of nausea returned in all its unsettling glory, but now it was accompanied by a light sprinkling of delight because I knew this time, no matter what I felt or how strongly I felt it, I would have to step off or be pushed after making that phone call.

CHAPTER 12

facing fear

'The fear will never go away, as long as I continue to grow'

SUSAN JEFFERS

In case you're curious, I hated the bungee jump and I never wanted to do one again, but that wasn't the point. In finally taking that voluntary step into a short but sickening free fall, I had experienced first hand that I could override my most potent fear and take the reins of rational choice. I knew now that, even while in its strongest grip, it was possible to control it rather than it controlling me. Once the aggressive rebounding of the cord and the accompanying stomach churn began to lose its force and momentum, I was absolutely elated that I'd jumped and was rewarded with an impressive natural high, the kind your body must reserve for the sudden absence of anticipated certain death. Comparing that feeling of extraordinary aliveness and pride with how I'd felt just hours earlier after giving in to panic and retreating to the safety of solid ground, I promised myself that from here on out, every opportunity I was presented with that in the past I would have said no to, I would now say yes.

My month of hightailing around Costa Rica in my trusty old banger had come to an end. With no plans or obligations I could choose to stay in the safety and comfort of this country I'd come to know and love – head back south to Santa Teresa Beach, back to the beautiful sunsets and the possibility of meeting another wandering shaman or another Yoni, a wishful repeat of what had been and gone. Or I could choose to keep stepping forward into the unexplored, leaving Costa Rica to head north across the border into Nicaragua and maybe onwards through Central America. The choice was an obvious one, but still it came coated in resistance, doubt and fear as I set off on the first of many long, hot bus journeys to come. I had already accepted that it was important to get comfortable with being uncomfortable. That the world and our lives within it are unpredictable and that there are mostly no right or wrong choices, only a different set of outcomes, setbacks and opportunities. In whatever would unfold over the coming months, with the certainty of constant change and new experiences, I could learn to control how I respond. In difficulty, I could gain resilience; in solitude, I could discover a more robust sense of self. And, of course, there were all the unspoken possibilities for wonder, for love and joy and freedom, for the people, places and adventures I couldn't yet imagine.

It was aboard that debut day-long bus ride from Costa Rica's capital, San José, to the popular coastal surf town of San Juan del Sur in Nicaragua that I had an obvious light-bulb moment that seemed to have eluded me up to that point. My phone had given up with six hours to go on the road, gone was my access to friends in faraway places, playlists, podcasts, articles or hours upon hours of mindless scrolling. When I'd been caught in that storm in Costa Rica without power or connection for four days this stream of thought had crossed my mind, but there was always a class or a person available to distract me. In the lonely, awkward confines of the bus it became clear to me through my own deep unease and frustration that I was utterly addicted to my phone and more specifically to social media. The inability to use my lifeless device highlighted just how often I reached for it and the now seemingly endless hours highlighted just how much of my time and attention it swallowed up. I was so uncomfortable sitting with only myself and the world passing by outside.

Up until that bus journey, even through all the hurt I'd been trying to untangle over the first months away from home, I'd still spent a chunk of my days capturing long happy-go-lucky Instagram stories, attempting to offer an insightful window into life on the road. For many years my career had felt increasingly bound to my online value, so it had become an engrained part of my daily life to share, and sometimes over-share, in the hopes that my small audience would deem me both likeable and engaging. It might sound ridiculous, but the light-bulb moment came when it occurred to me that I simply wasn't obliged to share anything at all ever again. I owed no one on the internet any part of my day. I'd walked away from the world in which this held any importance and all that mattered now was that *I* deemed *myself* to be likeable and engaging.

Good fucking riddance – you wouldn't believe the amount of subliminal stress this removed from my days or how much freedom I gained from excusing myself from this perceived duty. I remain far from free of the compulsion, but I have never used social media in the same way since. Instead of seeing it as a necessity or its feedback as a gauge of my social or professional value, it transitioned into a kind of scrapbook, a tool for sharing my genuine interests and a home for memories of a life well lived, which I will hopefully look back over one day with delight. It was a liberating re-evaluation of what exactly a 24-hour, 365-days-a-year connection to the whole world and seemingly everyone in it can do to your headspace. I was 29 years old when I had this epiphany, and I had been 16 before social media even existed. I thought I'd had ample opportunity to form a sense of self before it became commonplace for us to curate our outward personas based largely on the repetitive input of others mindlessly engaging with the contents of their personalised algorithm, but apparently not. Bear in mind, too, that I'd had the privilege of being on the aspirational side of social media, engaging with it as a model, an influencer and something of a travel blogger. But no matter what angle you're posting from, if you're a human being it is still inherently unhealthy to receive this kind of feedback every time you share an authentic, filtered or phony part of yourself. Add to that the ability to look through a distorted lens into hundreds or maybe thousands of other people's lives every day and it's bound to result in a social comparison that will leave you feeling like shit, regardless of how old you were when Bebo burst onto the dial-up. It's important to protect your peace in real life and online, and reawakening to my unconscious use of social media and choosing to change that daily pattern really helped me in that regard.

On another of my long trips, I was afforded the time to think through something else. Before I'd left home I worked nearly every day in the world of fashion and beauty, and while I really enjoyed getting styled in whatever expensive attire was due to be big for the coming season or being made up to feel beautiful and glamorous by skilled hair and make-up artists, it was always just work for me and nothing more – neither is something I care about on a personal level. I am fashion-challenged, to put it lightly, and my beauty regime consists of whatever requires the least possible effort for the best results. My staple look is now known as 'athleisure', I believe, but I just call it 'anything loose and comfortable' and I wear make-up, tan and all other enhancing trickery only when absolutely necessary. These things, which appear to hold such enormous currency in society, rate very low on my priority list and I'd always felt bad about that, like I was lazy or scruffy or gross, parading around with no regard for trends, with unwashed hair, flawed skin and significant eye bags unmasked. On the plus side it saved me a lot of money, but on the negative side I'd always felt this niggling need to look like I'd just walked straight off the cool, casual streets of Copenhagen with a subtle dewy contour and a loose blow-dry to fulfil the model-off-duty criteria, otherwise I wouldn't live up to people's expectations of me. I hated this pressure I felt to be perfect and pleasing to the eye at all times. This was, of course, my own insecurity, the story I told myself, and I'm sure no one cared whatsoever. Regardless, trying to look like someone I just wasn't remained a daily stressor. While travelling I got to live out of a bag that held minimal basic clothing options and a small selection of toiletries, and with just that I'd never felt more like myself. I was comfortable in the simplicity.

These moments of self-reflection may seem obvious, but to me they were a day-by-day release from the shackles of my old life and the burdens of my outdated thought processes. With every long, contemplative bus journey, I seemed to come closer to a less complicated, more authentic version of myself, and it felt good. With less came so much more.

Working my way up the spine of Central America over the course of a month, I found the time to read, reflect and experience more than I had for many, many years. I remember coming across a line in an online article titled 'The Purpose of Travelling' that summarised this feeling of shedding so well: 'The point of all this has nothing to do with finding yourself. It's about what you, as a temporary traveller, can do to lose what you don't need.' In this small window of time living as an anonymous backpacker lost somewhere in the world, I could drop the physical and metaphorical baggage I'd acquired to enhance my identity in my normal life. I could take my sense of self back to basics and see what I found there, escape my inhibitions, my biases, my social conditioning and, of course, my fear.

All this said, it would be misleading to imply that I'd somehow blossomed into a pensive guru type, because I absolutely had not – this was the very early stages of elementary insight, and I was still mostly a bumbling mess running on hope and intuition. In the larger scale of things, these moments were few and fleeting, nestled like gems among the familiar chaos of risky decisions, hangovers and self-doubt. Nevertheless, they stayed with me and contributed to a slow change over time. And I was aware of a feeling of expansion during this period, an ever-growing sense of self-confidence that kept me just brave enough to continue on each new quest. In every country I would seek out anxiety-inducing situations and force myself to step up to them and embrace whatever unfolded. This was my self-prescribed medicine, a remedy born from intuition and a means of learning to cope with, or maybe eventually conquer, the demon that had stopped me in my tracks only months earlier. I was growing to trust in my capacity to look after myself, to make the right call for me, to manage the little daily hurdles and recurring tasks of travel on my own, navigating foreign border crossings or getting around countries when I didn't speak the native language.

° ° °

On leaving Nicaragua's pristine coastline, I headed inland to hike to the top of Cerro Negro, a steep active volcano just outside the city of León. It is covered in sharp, loose deep-black volcanic shrapnel, and the plan for the morning was to board down it at high speed from the exposed ridge on its summit. On a normal day I've heard that the hike is quiet pleasant once you have a baseline level of fitness, but the day I climbed it there was a torrential storm with thick, low cloud cover, pelting rain and high speed winds. If this had been anywhere else, health and safety regulations may have been taken into consideration, but our local guide plodded steadily on with his board held solidly on his shoulders. Mine, however, seemed to be acting as large wooden wings and I almost took flight with every hefty gust of wind.

On arrival at the ridge, with the unguarded drop into the volcano's crater, thankfully filled with cloud, to our right and the steep descent to ground level to our left, we had to burrow down into a close huddle many times until each strong gust eased slightly, allowing us to proceed precariously onward to the highest point, known as 'the drop zone'. Deciding to join in these types of activities was supposed to be a relatively enjoyable way to keep chipping away at my fear, but it seemed the universe kept handing me the most undesirable versions of it to overcome. Shaking through the familiar internal screams of resistance, damp to my bones and battling to stay upright in a slicing wind, I absolutely did not want to push myself off the edge of this ridge into the uncertainty of the cloud cover below.

The drop to the base takes on average 45 seconds and, depending on some law of physics or luck, your board can reach speeds of up to 50 miles per hour – maybe more in this rain, I thought. People come off regularly, tumbling at speed over the sharp volcanic sand that slices through skin like glass. Cue a repeat of the cycle of catastrophic thoughts I'd had before the bungee jump, except this time I would not under any circumstances turn back. Reminded of the disappointment I'd felt when I'd caved in to the fear, I told myself it just wasn't an option: the only way down to the warmth of the van below was on this board, otherwise I'd have to live on this volcano ridge, cold and wet, forever. I dug my heels into the earth and rallied myself off that edge with absolute commitment and not once did I allow my feet to drag on the gravel to slow my descent. In an instant it was over, my face black from the spray-back and my heart thumping, those delicious endorphins making their way into my bloodstream, but this time with the bonus that I'd actually enjoyed myself in the process! It seemed I'd managed to not only overcome the fear, but also somehow let it go on the way down. I was beginning to understand why people do this stuff to themselves. Fear might never leave us, but maybe through exposure, investigation and ultimately acceptance or surrender, it can be transformed into something we even look forward to as a prerequisite for the high. This was an encouraging notion I chose to adopt for continued motivation.

Pushing north and ever further away from my comfort zone, I lived with a Mayan family in a homestay on Lake Atitlán, talked my way out of bribes imposed by chancers masquerading as government officials at the El Salvadorian border and spent Halloween in Honduras drinking too much guifiti, a blend of herbs and spices mixed with liquor and touted locally for its healing powers. Reaching Guatemala with a banging headache and feeling far from healed, I took on the most gruelling hike I could find, a single-day 12-hour slog to a 4,000-metre elevation at the peak of Acatenango. There I sat above the clouds to watch its neighbour, the Fuego volcano, spit and spew burning lava. In Belize I trekked in nauseating heat and humidity to the entrance of the most claustrophobic and advanced caving expedition I could find as a beginner.

After seven hours underground, clambering downward using ropes and the single beam from my head torch, contorting our bodies to pass through small cracks in the cave wall and traversing slippery horizontal rock that seemed to disappear downward into complete nothingness, we were filthy, exhausted and a long, long way from sunshine or civilisation when we finally arrived in Wonderland, a sparkling expanse of crystal cave that turned my pounding adrenaline to pure awe. The floor, the ceiling and every grand formation created millimetre by millimetre over millions of years glistened brightly, even in total blackness. Describing in words the beauty, the scale and the feeling of standing in the heart of something this otherworldly is impossible, and this in itself only added to my growing certainty that everything good and worthwhile can be found on the other side of fear.

From the heart of the Belizean jungle, I boarded a rickety chicken bus headed for Belize City and from there I had plans to catch an afternoon boat to the laid-back Caribbean island of Caye Caulker, where the local motto is 'Go Slow'. It felt only right to intersperse these expeditions to the edge of my tolerance for petrification with long bouts of lying undisturbed on as many white sandy beaches as possible. A fellow gringo boarded the chaos of the bus and we caught eyes briefly before he took the empty seat beside me, one of the last free spots in a growing sea of bodies. 'Hi there – a backpacker too, I presume?' he opened with as soon as he sat down.

Fear comes in many shapes and sizes – bungee jumping or forcing yourself into tight, dark spaces deep underground could be considered universal triggers, but so, too, is the less acknowledged fear of social judgement or isolation. In hindsight, the amount of time I spent alone was a very important part of my journey, but it is also one of the main obstacles for people when it comes to travelling solo – the assumption of loneliness and the associated fear of putting ourselves out there to meet new people as a remedy. In the routine of our regular lives, we may not make a new friend for years – just going about our days, we're often stressed, probably tired and certainly not trying with any great effort to add to our inner circle. So this aspect of travel is intimidating because we are comparing it to the social norms of our usual routine, in which it would most likely be odd to strike up a conversation with a stranger on the bus with the hidden agenda of perhaps accompanying them to wherever they're going next. But backpacking isn't normal life and neither is the way you form friendships. Even though it seemed implausible to me before I was on the road, they really do come easy. And when you're the only foreigners on a hot, rattling chicken bus so filled to capacity that the locals have to hang from ledges on the bus's exterior, there are quite a few options to break the ice.

He was from Wales, travelling alone for six months through Central America. This was just day two of his trip and it also happened to be his birthday. His final destination for the day was Caye Caulker too, and just like that I had a companion for the rest of the journey and plans to celebrate into the night. Staying in hostel dorm rooms generally means you have to actively try to spend time alone. Even with that guarantee of company, I had expected to often feel lonely, but I found that I collected comforting connections with like-minded people as easily as I collected mosquito bites because our paths were crossing on a shared experience. Some I will stay in touch with for a lifetime, others I travelled with for months, weeks, days or maybe just hours before we parted ways. The point being, of all the muddled fears I harboured at the outset of this journey, this one left me the quickest.

In practising the art of meeting new people every other day, I found a real gratitude for my Irishness and the culturally engrained ease with which we banter. As a nation we're warm, open, fun and easily befriended, and one of the greatest gifts I assimilated from this time is the acceptance that I am all of the above in abundance. It was like I unfurled in that regard, became less nervous and protected, allowed myself to be totally authentic and found a social seal of approval in response – and even the need for that fell away as I began to trust my own ability to connect with others in a meaningful way and form lasting friendships. This alone has been an invaluable change that has expanded and improved my life ever since.

However, as well as a reluctant, burgeoning explorer of my inner world, I was still very much an impulsive delinquent. That night, like so many other nights, myself, my new Welsh friend and a bunch of other new acquaintances from our hostel ventured out into the uncharted possibilities, following the sounds of reggae to a beach bar where we could snort bad cocaine in the rotting wooden outdoor toilets and drink cocktails so sweet they made our taste-buds ache. What was unusual about this night is that I had a one-night stand on a pier with the Welsh man after we decided that skinny-dipping by moonlight was the best possible idea, perhaps driven by notions of living out a scene from one of the many popular romcoms of our youth. I was getting better at forming deep connections and I could certainly have opted to explore my sexual identity as part of this year of liberation and self-discovery, but this was my lone tale of frivolity, as I discovered the following morning that I'd grown out of my ability to engage in casual, meaningless sex. It just did not make me feel good and I knew

I couldn't afford the knocks to my sense of well-being, so I took note and decided it was at least something ticked off the bucket list. We stayed friends, of course, and he was extremely encouraging, although entirely closed to invitation, when I told him I was considering scuba-diving with sharks the following day, the next step up the ladder on my itinerary of terror. 'I'll walk you to the dock,' he'd offered, and yet again I readied myself to face the challenge alone.

Belize is one of the most beautiful places in the world to scuba-dive and one of the cheapest places to get your Professional Association of Diving Instructors (PADI) certificate, something I was considering staying on to do if I enjoyed the experience.

I'd had a debilitating fear of putting my head underwater without holding my nose since I was a kid, so scuba-diving filled me with dread, as did the small issue of the sharks – and nothing could have prepared me for how many there were. I suppose I should have guessed when our captain informed us that we would be anchoring at 'shark alley' for the next hour. Schools of them surrounded the boat as far as the eye could see as our guide enthusiastically flung himself backwards into the ocean without hesitation. I was ready for the familiar pangs of dread, the dry mouth, the sweaty extremities, the urge to dash to the bathroom and, of course, the mental showcase of every reason I shouldn't get in that water, and as predicted, they arrived in alarming unison like a marching band as I closed my eyes tight and fell backwards, telling myself the dip would be good for the hang-over. I got through it but certainly lost that briefly uncovered ability to let go of the fear in the process – for the entire hour I was acutely aware of how alien the environment was and how vulnerable I felt in it. At one point some water got into my mouthpiece and I couldn't seem to purge it even with multiple attempts, so I panicked and fled swiftly and without thinking to the surface without releasing my breath on the way up, which really hurt my lungs – I do not recommend it. After that I switched to snorkelling, staying at surface level, and found myself easing into the sharks' constant slow-moving company. Again, in spite of the fear and all its unwelcome warning signs, I hadn't died. But I did decide against the PADI cert for now and instead made plans to cross the border into Mexico.

CHAPTER 13

falling in love in peru

'And in the middle of my chaos, there was you'

PAULLINA SIMONS

Is it possible to be so self-aware that you become absorbed with yourself to the point of lacking all self-awareness?

This thought crossed my mind as I cycled along the narrow, rustic, palm tree-fringed road that runs parallel to Tulum's stretch of pure paradise beach. Hayley, one of my closest friends from home, had come to join me on my travels for an undetermined amount of time, and I decided this might be a good opportunity to ease up on the self-analysis and enjoy a little carefree fun. By now my anxiety had almost outright dissolved compared to how it used to plague me. I still battled with off days, when I felt I couldn't get a handle on it and I'd rather stay in bed, but those were mostly in perfect correlation with my self-inflicted hang-overs.

Having spent the guts of a week lazing on the beach and doing not much else, we'd befriended an oceanfront-resort manager who began to reserve us a lounge bed and bring us the half-empty bottles of wine left over from their lunch-time 'food and wine pairing' experience. We were staying in a hostel in Tulum town, half an hour's cycle from the renowned bohemian allure and affluence of the beach area. Our damp, dark room was the closest I've come to the experience of sleeping in a prison cell, so this taste of how the other half lived was very welcome. On our last day, with flights booked to fly to Mexico City the following afternoon, our favourite manager extended an invitation to the hotel's Thanksgiving celebrations that evening, 'An invite-only five-course meal by the ocean with access to a free bar for the duration of the service,' he'd explained. We might have played it cool in response if we hadn't drunk the equivalent of a few bottles of wine each by then, so instead, with squeals of glee, we wholeheartedly accepted the offer. The meal was exquisite, as were the many,

many shots of aged mescal, and now a little more than merry, dressed in our best backpacker glad rags, Hayley and I decided to head out to one of Tulum's beautiful jungle bars to dance beneath the disco balls dangling from palm trees. Lost to the influence of tequila and swaying to some very alternative instrumental folk/house mash-up, I literally bumped into a familiar face from home, an acquaintance I knew through mutual friends who I'd heard had upped and moved to this beautiful part of the world on a whim and a notion.

Prior to this meeting, I'd decided against letting him know I was in the same small town, mainly because I didn't see the point in dragging him through an awkward coffee where he'd feel obliged to show me around until he could politely excuse himself. I thought we'd have absolutely nothing in common outside of our nationality because on first impressions he seemed to care about everything that I absolutely didn't. From afar, he'd struck me as a sports-car-revving, designer-shoes-and-belt kind of guy, who probably had aspirations for a trophy wife to accessorise his trophy life. I'd seen online that he also had a perfectly chiselled six pack and sometimes wore those tiny stringy bodybuilder vests that show off maximum upper body muscle with intermittent flashes of nipple, which led me to also assume that his company would be rather uninspiring, an unfair association probably rooted in envy. But I had to admit that, in person, dressed in a regular old T-shirt, he was cute. Hayley echoed those sentiments with the drunken encouragement, 'Talk to him, dammit – he's hot.'

We got chatting over the blare of pretentious music and within the first 30 minutes I was riddled with guilt for being so judgemental. He seemed perfectly lovely, charming even. So I made a mental note to add this impulse to label others to the long list of 'shit I need to fix about myself' and opened up to the idea of a blossoming friendship between us. The night was immensely good fun, as was he, with a constant flow of drinks convincing us all to make our presence felt on the dance floor until we were practically asked to leave. On retreating to the beach in the early hours of the morning, I heard him give an impromptu, impassioned speech about American right-wing politics and how it had become unpopular to remotely align oneself with even its more reasonable policies. I can't say we bonded over our shared views in this regard, but I was impressed with how articulate he was, even after far too many drinks and in spite of parting with his money for those stringy vests. But with the conversation getting a little heavy, perhaps, his friend suggested more drinks at his hotel and the night rolled on.

I woke some time in the afternoon of the following day to Hayley informing me, 'We've missed our flight to Mexico City' and 'You got into a fight with his friend back at the hotel and started crying, so I took you home.' Just a reminder, I was a 29-year-old woman flinging around judgement like it was nobody's business. That afternoon, with our onward flights rebooked and all seemingly forgiven from the night before, we met for recovery tacos on the beach and I just couldn't shake a growing sense of attachment and the feeling that I did not want to leave this man. In my delicate state, his confident, assertive masculinity felt magnetic, protective, like a very safe place. I tried not to let my mind dwell on this, but sometimes, when I was sick of being strong and tired of being alone, I couldn't help but indulge in the romantic idea that someone like him would swoop into my life, a knight in shining armour to make it all better like the Disney movies of my youth had promised. But as I'd known him properly for about 12 hours, made a questionable impression and was now leaving, I decided not to get my hopes up.

Hayley and I had made plans to fly from Mexico City back to Panama at the base of Central America, where this whole trip had started. From Panama we'd arrange to sail through the San Blas Islands into northern Colombia. My travel route was a disorganised, convoluted mess, just like me. So I reassured myself that by tomorrow this hang-over-induced neediness would be gone and in a few days this man would return to acquaintance status, with the addition of a one-off tale of a good night spent dancing together in the jungles of Tulum. Turning that quiet niggle for more into gratitude for what was made it easier to say goodbye later that day, and getting onto the plane, I never expected to hear from him again outside of some obligatory pleasantries.

Hayley and I only had a long weekend to explore Mexico City, which mainly centred around any Freda Kahlo-themed sights interspersed with bartering our way through the city's many impressive markets, and on arrival in Panama City it was much of the same jam-packed tourist agenda on top of organising our boat trip through the archipelago just off the coast. With all the running around I hadn't spoken to or thought of him much, until he sent me a message reminding me that I was probably so eager to visit the San Blas Islands because of him. We'd been friends on Instagram for a while, and over a year earlier I had voyeuristically watched him take a motorbike trip through Central and South America, commenting enthusiastically on his pictures and videos from the San Blas Islands. I'd completely forgotten about this brief interaction in the fog of the year that had passed, but I had to give credit where credit was due: it *was* because of him that I'd come to know that this small, remote, entirely disconnected tropical paradise even existed. And with that simple reminder, he became an honorary tour guide from afar, arming us with regular tips and tricks for our upcoming stops.

Leaving Panama we sailed from tiny island to tiny island, each its own miniature utopia providing the choice to nap in your hammock suspended between the palms, dip in the clear-blue placid waters or enjoy the freshly caught lobster and cracked coconuts provided by the wonderfully welcoming indigenous Kuna tribe who independently govern this blissful region.

The San Blas is made up of hundreds of small palm-covered islands dotted along the coast of Panama's notoriously dangerous and dense stretch of jungle known as the Darién Gap. It is impassable by road or on foot, unless you're a narcotics trafficker, a member of a rebel army or the owner of an off-road vehicle and a death wish, so passing into neighbouring Colombia can only be done by water or by air, and after four heavenly disconnected days on the sea, I was giddy to chat to the man who'd drawn me to this incredible place to gush over the shared experience.

His name was Dave and over the next month he virtually accompanied Hayley and me from place to place along the northern coastline of Colombia. We stopped in every rural beach town, lusciously green national park and colourful city, hiking a testing four days to the ancient Lost City high in the Sierra Nevada de Santa Marta mountains and exploring the rolling hippy hills of Minca before heading inland to the city of Medellín and all its surrounding beauty. The list of things to do and places to see along the typical backpacker route was endless so our days were always full, and I enjoyed everything so much more when I knew I could tell him all about it at the end of the day. What had started as a couple of practical texts and general chatter soon transitioned into short but detailed phone calls every evening, and then those phone calls began to last well into the early hours of the following morning, which didn't go unnoticed by Hayley: 'Oh God, he's texted you for a chat, hasn't he? You have that stupid smile on your face again.' Without any effort at all, this man I'd spent less than 24 hours with in person began to feel like my best friend in world – although I'm not sure it's normal to get butterflies in your stomach when your best friend's name pops up on your phone.

Even though he was thousands of miles away, he came to feel like a constant source of comfort, guidance and care. For instance, when I mentioned in passing that my phone was overheating to the point of almost melting in my hand and probably about to implode, he posted his outdated, unused model to my hostel, saving me a whole host of hassle and expense. Or when I got food poisoning and ended up bed-bound for a couple of days, we chatted for nearly 24 hours straight, barely letting sleep get in the way of conversation. He became the person I'd turn to to make me laugh and feel better when I'd wake up feeling like hell after yet another night of taking far too much cocaine and drinking far too many shots, encouraging me to ease up on the partying and get out into the day. It felt so normal and right to have acquired this faraway confidant.

Alongside this budding relationship inside my phone, Hayley and I had had the best couple of months adventuring through Panama, Colombia and into northern Peru, meeting new friends and making new memories along the way, but she decided it was time for her to leave and head back to work in her temporary home of New Zealand, leaving me once more on my own. On one of our last days together we went sandboarding and dune-buggying in Peru's Huacachina Desert, the first activity in a while to induce that familiar feeling of heart-thumping fear, and I'd sort of missed it. That evening, like every evening, I spoke to Dave on the phone for hours, telling him about Hayley's planned departure and my intentions to get back on the bandwagon of scaring myself as often as possible as I worked my way down through South America, and I thought no more of it as I finally fell asleep, far too late as usual. The next morning I woke to an email from him containing flight details and a note that he would meet me in Cusco in just a couple of days to travel with me for a few weeks. I was simultaneously annoyed and overwhelmed in response – annoyed because I wasn't given the chance to decide if I wanted to spend every minute of the day living in the pocket of this man I barely knew in person and overwhelmed because, in spite of that, it was the most romantic gesture I'd ever been shown. I was apprehensive and giddy at the thought of his arrival, but decided to use the next day's 18-hour bus journey to Cusco to mull it over and prepare myself.

We had our first date sitting on the balcony of a small café overlooking the Plaza de Armas, the beautiful colonial centre of this unique red-roofed city. Once the capital of the Inca Empire, it sits in a valley eclipsed in all directions by the rolling peaks of the Peruvian Andes, and it was while wandering its narrow labyrinth of quaint cobblestoned streets to nowhere that we finally got to chat for hours in person. 'Let's go to Machu Picchu tomorrow,' he'd suggested as we strolled, and so it came to be that we had our first kiss the following day hidden somewhere among the clouds and morning mist that falls over the vertical green cliffs that house these truly breath-taking, otherworldly ruins – considered by many to be the energetic heart of the world. You couldn't write a more perfect fairy-tale beginning for a love story or imbue it with more potential prosperity than that, and our first kiss literally left me breathless. It was like nothing I had experienced before in my life, and not just on account of the impeccable setting. I could hardly control the childlike regression I was experiencing – I was giddy and playful on account of the flood of feel-good hormones. In person he was everything I had imagined him to be over all those hours of texts and calls – in fact, he was proving to be so much more and I was helplessly falling, floating or whatever you want to call it. I was deliriously happy.

In complete contrast to my initial perceptions, we seemed to have everything in common and each day spent together was more exhilarating than the last. Aware of my love of nature, fondness for a hike and hopes to overcome my fears through stubborn repeated exposure, he hit the ground running with his tour-guide tips for optional excursions. We slogged together through thin air up the steep, soggy earth that leads to the vivid turquoise magic of Humantay Lake. Found along the Inca trail high in the Peruvian Andes and enclosed by snow-capped peaks that soar into the sky, it looked like a green-screen projection, a landscape almost unbelievable to the naked eye. We rented a car for a day to explore the expanse of the Sacred Valley and the many small rural villages nestled amid Peru's sublime countryside on the road to the base of the Technicolor natural phenomenon that is Rainbow Mountain, crossing rapid mud-red streams and waving to farming families carrying home their piles of harvest in their brightly patterned traditional dress. 'You have to try this,' he told me as he pulled the car over at a roadside stall. Having travelled through Peru before, he was excited to introduce me to Inca Kola – 'the pride of the Peruvian nation', apparently – a strange kind of clear green liquid that tastes exactly like Coca-Cola. I loved these little insights he offered so regularly and the opportunity to share these experiences with someone so much that I had to stop myself from drowning in the hope of what it could be and drag myself back to simply enjoying the moment over and over.

We were entirely alone on the Rainbow Mountain trail, with the exception of some llamas or the odd decorated donkey or local farmer at work, and we cheered each other on to the remarkable views at the top, sitting to rest and take it all in at 5,200 metres above sea level. I told him on our descent that I hoped to one day beat my proudly held 'personal record' of 5,895 metres, which I'd reached at the summit of Kilimanjaro all those years ago while filming that series taking the piss out of models trying to be outdoorsy. A few toenails were lost and a few tantrums were had, but we all made it to the tip of Africa's highest mountain and it was still one of my proudest achievements.

'Are you ready to leave Cusco?' he asked me the following day, and I knew he had something in mind when he suggested our next stop should be La Paz in Bolivia, the world's highest capital city. Allowing him to take the reins on my travel plans for a few weeks felt like being swept off my feet and swaddled all at once. I trusted him, which was not a default feeling for me, and so with every passing day my guard dropped more and my scepticism about this unfamiliar and sudden situation eased. We spent our first night in Bolivia acclimatising to the altitude at a Cholita wrestling show high in the El Alto region of the city, a bizarre event where two indigenous women dressed in full skirts, fringed shawls and traditional Bolivian bowler hats fling each other around a ring WWE-style while the crowd of mostly backpackers roars and throws popcorn at them. A theatrical treat you'll find nowhere else in the world, but a misleading introduction for what was to come. I wanted fear and La Paz has no shortage of options in that regard.

First on the agenda was a tourist favourite, Death Road, a downhill rally 60 kilometres long, with a 3,500-metre descent, lacking in any health or safety precautions. Your bike has brakes, of course, so you could have controlled fun the whole way to the bottom, but Dave took off like a professional mountain biker, skidding into sharp corners and skimming the edge of the terrifying vertical cliff drop that was ever present to our left. I have a bubbling but somewhat manageable fear when it comes to heights. I have an intense, consuming fear when it comes to falling. Falling to my death haunts me in my dreams, so that cliff drop had me truly shaken to start with. For the first few kilometres I was cautious, taking full advantage of the brakes, and in doing so I noticed that I was actually making the whole thing harder. The ground was covered in loose, damp grit and gravel, which meant speed, counterintuitively, seemed to give you a little more control, while progressing like a snail seemed to mean every bump or pothole could derail your wheels. With Dave at the front of the pack I decided to go for it, partly to impress him, and after a few shaky minutes I was absolutely buzzing, surprising myself with the speed and confidence I quickly clocked up, eventually passing Dave and rallying onwards into every blind twist and turn the whole way to the bottom. I'd come to love the feeling of adrenaline you're rewarded with as and after you overcome fear, and still soaring on its effects that evening, I was certain I could take on Dave's next exciting suggestion: a 6,088-metre climb to the precarious ridged summit of Huayna Potosí, an ice-capped mountain that towers over La Paz.

I loved to hike and climb mountains, but this would be my first ascent with any element of technicality, requiring us to take a half day's training to get comfortable with our crampons, ice axes, ropes, harnesses and excesses of gear. It would take three days up and another day down, but was advertised as accessible to beginners, so I was ready to conquer new heights as we set off to the mountain's base with our seasoned guide. Bearing in mind that this was Bolivia, one of

South America's poorest countries, with pockets of extreme poverty visible even in the bustling city of La Paz, advertising this climb as suitable for beginners may have been slightly misleading in the hopes of attracting extra numbers, and I can now confirm that it is *not* suitable! After three days of a slow and steady upward slog, with Dave powering through on a dodgy tummy while often carrying my bag as well as his own, we arrived at the summit night lodge, where we were fed and told to get a few hours' sleep before we made a final push under cover of night to reach the top for sunrise. 'You'll have a new personal record by the morning,' Dave enthused through the discomfort of his stomach pain, his encouragement unrelenting. I hadn't yet realised how much I often relied on the encouragement or permission of others to tap into my own innate capacity.

The hike was brutal, the air thin and temperatures below freezing. My body felt like a deadweight, so I could only imagine how Dave was feeling. Just 400 metres shy of the top, we arrived at an almost vertical and terrifyingly narrow stretch of path carved into the ice on the sheer mountainside. There was a vertical drop into nothing but darkness on our right and a deep, hollow crevasse that ate a chunk out of the already thin path to our left, further obstructing the terrifying only way forward. I went first, and with my crampons shakily forced into the ice to keep me upright while looking for the next point to slam my ice axe, before I'd even registered what was happening I was in the grips of pure panic (extra fun at high altitude, where breathing is already laboured). Dave and our guide had to pry me off the cliff face and down to a wider ledge, legs trembling, wailing and gasping for air. We'd made it to 5,750 metres, just 150 metres below that Kilimanjaro record. I calmed down quickly in the security of Dave's arms, but our guide wouldn't even entertain a conversation about me giving that section another shot, as the 400 metres above that paralysing ridge apparently continued gifting vertigo-inducing surprises. He decided I wasn't ready or able to go on, so we turned back and headed for the lodge having failed because of me. I felt so guilty, especially considering Dave had made it that far in spite of being so unwell, but he couldn't have been more comforting, kind or reassuring in the face of my disappointment, promising we'd come back one day with a little more practice to defeat that ridge, and perhaps delighted he could finally get some sleep too.

Our time together after that experience returned to being magical and, thankfully, a little less life-threatening. From La Paz we continued south to the Uyuni salt flats, a dry lake basin of pure white rock salt as far as the eye can see. When it rains, the surface of the earth perfectly mirrors the sky, capturing you in the centre – it's the closest thing to heaven on earth. The only visual stimulus that disrupts the vast emptiness of the flats is sparsely located small islands of densely packed cacti or beautiful flocks of pink flamingos, and this ethereal world of natural wonders was all we'd know for the next four days as we hopped in a 4x4 to journey across the Bolivian Altiplano into the deserts of northern Chile.

This is the world's highest desert plateau, awash with volcanoes, sulphur lakes, iridescent pink, purple and turquoise lagoons, surreal thermal hot springs and sprawling displays of steamy geysers that make you feel like you've arrived on Mars, all nestled in the endless surrounds of multihued desert. It is another world, the most astonishing array of landscapes in the absolute middle of nowhere, and I got to experience it with this incredible person by my side. It was movie-worthy, and I couldn't quite wrap my head around my luck. On one occasion we pulled over at the edge of a brightly coloured lagoon, home to flocks of flamingos and backdropped by deep purple hills and tall, almost cartoon-shaped volcanoes, to eat lunch. I remember looking at him and thinking *there's no going back now* – after experiencing all of this together, how could I ever start over with anyone else? I would be bound to a lifetime of hopelessly attempting to recreate these impossible highs, and that realisation scared me more than the panic-inducing ridge on Huayna Potosí. I recognised the urge to protect myself, to push him away, but I had learned from my mistakes and I would not let some underlying fear of rejection or uncertainty or whatever it was make me cold again. I would be myself, soft, open and kind, in all its gloriously petrifying vulnerability.

Crossing the border into Chile, we arrived in the Atacama Desert, the driest, clearest place on earth and the world's best stargazing location. With plans to enjoy the famously bright night skies, roam the moon-like landscape and float in some baby-blue lakes with higher salinity than the Dead Sea, I was looking forward to our last few days together, even though I never wanted this time to come to an end. At that point I didn't think it was possible to be any more smitten with a man I'd only known a few weeks, and I was trying my best to play it cool. Having met in Mexico, I knew he could speak almost perfect Spanish, which had been a great aid while navigating South America, but on check-in to our last hotel he suddenly started conversing in fluent French with the Parisian employee behind the desk. There was no more fighting it. I crumbled hopelessly in love. Any rationality was lost and I became a woman possessed, mentally pairing his last name with my own and picturing our unborn children.

In only a month together, we had travelled through three countries, four if you count the one we met in, and travelling together is a fast track to discovering how compatible you really are with a person – multiply the effects tenfold when you're backpacking. In that short but intense window, on top of creating a list of once-in-a-lifetime memories, we'd already handled the monstrous versions of each other that can creep out during long commuting days and weathered tummy bugs with all their undignified manifestations. In fact, on one unfortunate occasion, while lying in an ill-considered tangle, I'd farted practically on his head. Instead of getting to the point where I revealed myself without make-up, I don't think he ever saw me with a scrap of make-up on. But he definitely got to see me cranky, hungry, tired, sweaty, flustered, moaning over a breakout and everything in between. There was no honeymoon stage. We'd gone from zero to one hundred, lived in each other's company 24/7, without privacy or peace, and loved it. And I loved more than just that: I loved how my hand was so small in his that we could only intertwine our pinkie fingers; I loved the now-familiar coil we would assume in bed at night and how easily I slept because of it; I loved the back of his head when he walked in front of me; I loved his pimples, his feet and the deep furrow in his brow when he got irritated. Even though we'd spoken for hours every day for weeks on end and done, seen and overcome more together than I had with some people I'd known for decades, I could barely justify the magnitude of my feelings when I considered how ridiculous the timeframe was. But the potential for our future was enthusiastically shared and I wanted to allow myself to believe in it rather than run from it.

We flew together to Santiago, where he was catching a flight home and I was preparing myself for the goodbye and to be alone once again with the open road to anywhere in front of me. Because of the sickening feeling of impending loss rising in my stomach, I wanted to ask him to stay and then seriously considered just following him back to Mexico where we could live happily ever after, but I knew neither was a realistic option. He had to get back to work and, as far as he was concerned, I had the whole world to explore yet. But more than that, I knew I had to tend to my own business and figure out what I'd left home to figure out before I could offer anything to anyone else. So for now until sometime soon, with all our budding feelings and defiant commitment to each other expressed, we reluctantly kissed goodbye on the steps of my hostel and my heart broke as he walked away. I had never expected to be left feeling like this or to cry myself to sleep in my dorm room that night, missing him desperately. But the tears were happy ones, sourced from gratitude for this unexpected twist in my story, and I began to count the days until we would meet again.

CHAPTER 14

know thyself

'The curious paradox is that when I accept myself just as I am, then I can change'

CARL ROGERS

I had acquired a lot of unconscious self-soothing techniques throughout my life. For instance, in an uncomfortable, usually confrontational situation, when I couldn't simply excuse myself, storm off or mentally vacate the room, I would sit with my legs and arms tightly crossed to protect my body while fidgeting with or covering the area around my mouth with my hand. I would automatically turn to grazing on food as a distraction when I got bored, sad or overwhelmed, and if I didn't want to feel an emotion I would just keep busy, which could take many healthy or unhealthy outward forms like working too much, drinking, taking drugs, a hectic travel schedule, cleaning and organising my life. After Dave left, I felt acutely down and alone, even in the surrounds of a busy city like Santiago so I headed straight for the colourful graffiti town of Valparaíso – a street artist's mecca offering a labyrinth of beautiful, bright streets to get lost in – and the long stretches of beach in the more affluent neighbouring Viña del Mar to explore, meet new people and finalise my plans to fly to Rio de Janeiro in Brazil in the coming days.

Everyone I had met and kept in touch with so far while backpacking through Central and South America was heading there to reconvene for the infamous Rio Carnival festival. It would be 10 days of endless, gorgeous, glittering debauchery, joining daytime street parties known as *blocos* to parade raucous and sweaty through the high cobbled streets of Santa Teresa and roll over into the night on the beautiful beaches of Copacabana or Ipanema. It was the exact prescription I needed for my feelings of heartbreak and aloneness, as well as a potential remedy for having involuntarily fallen in love. I wanted to push it away, dull the sense of vulnerability and return to the safety of not caring so much because no one could hurt me there.

I looked up the flights from Santiago to Rio multiple times a day for many days in a row while texting back and forth about accommodation and other plans with all my friends who were there or due to be there soon, but something felt off in the pit of my stomach, which was not like me. Generally impulsive and immediate in my actions, I knew I was simply repeating the unhelpful patterns I'd adhered to my whole adult life, and that was the opposite of the point of this year away. In going to Rio I was letting myself down and I could feel it. It also occurred to me during this unusual period of indecision that those few weeks I had spent with Dave had been my longest duration of sobriety since leaving home over half a year earlier. Maybe because of that, something in my gut had the space to surface and was now willing me to continue to choose courage over comfort, to do what was right for me instead of what was fun, fast or easy and to practise the values I held instead of just thinking that I held them. 'Who am I when I'm alone with myself?' It felt right to dig deep to answer that question now, more right than continuing to run and hide from it. So with little to no research, no planning whatsoever and the absolute basics in terms of appropriate gear, I booked a flight south to the vast nothingness of Tierra del Fuego, the end of the earth.

Even though it features prominently on many a bucket list, trekking through Patagonia, the continent's wild and mountainous southern frontier, was never something I dreamed I would or could do. It hadn't made it anywhere near my made-up-as-I-go-along itinerary because I thought it was too scary for a girl alone and unguided, and far too expensive for a backpacker's budget. I had no idea what I would find there, how long I would stay or how I would fill my time. But as I kept learning over and over, when you listen to your authentic intuition, the universe has a way of unfolding in your favour.

My flight left me in the remote tin-roofed town of Punta Arenas on the southernmost tip of Chile, sitting right on the edge of the Strait of Magellan, which connects the Atlantic and Pacific Oceans. I learned on check-in to the only hostel in the area that it is generally the likes of *National Geographic* photographers or hard-core wildlife enthusiasts that make the trip to this obscure place to observe the straits' many beautiful inhabitants. Other than that, sailors or scientists use the town as a base for their excursions to Antarctica. *Great*, I thought, *I fit right in, so*. My facial expression must have conveyed a plea for help or an indication that I was somewhat lost in the world because the very kind lady who owned the hostel quickly directed me to her communal dining table and brought me hot tea and a pamphlet containing information about a tour to Isla Magdalena. 'This,' she told me, 'is something you could start with to find your feet and it will be leaving early in the morning.'

If anywhere could have dispelled my feelings about Patagonia being an intimidating, unwelcoming place, it was Isla Magdalena. A tiny 200-acre island off the coast of Punta Arenas, its only inhabitants are an estimated 120,000 penguins – or, more accurately, 58,000 adorable and very loyal penguin couples who come here annually to mate, locating each other in the flock with a unique song only they share. Docking on this unassuming rocky enclave protruding from the choppy waters, I saw penguins everywhere – an unfathomable number of tiny, heart-melting penguins, none of which seemed to have developed any fear of humans and were curious and brave enough to waddle right under my feet. As if that wasn't enough, on our two-hour sail back to the mainland we passed an impressively large sea-lion colony, filling the shores of a neighbouring island to capacity to bask in the afternoon sunshine, and a pair of majestic humpback whales blowing geysers into the air and flapping their enormous tails in near unison. The waters here are free from predators and rich in krill and plankton so apparently this type of sighting is commonplace, but I could barely contain the overspill of privilege and excitement. Patagonia was my place – I was meant to be there. Bathed in nature and large open spaces, I felt myself ease into a sense of peace and flow.

Invigorated by this feeling of belonging, I considered continuing further south and across the border into Argentina to do some of the hiking trails around Ushuaia's steep icy peaks or to take that coveted picture at the sign in Tierra del Fuego National Park, the official end of the earth. I also took a notion about trying to secure one of the last-minute spots aboard a vessel headed across the notoriously rough stretch of ocean known as the Drake Passage to the tip of the Antarctic Peninsula to explore the most remote expanse on earth before returning the same sketchy route about 10 days later. I got myself very worked up and committed to this idea until I learned that even a last-minute allocation can set you back about seven grand. Quickly relegating it to the 'one day' wish list of my life, I took a 10 quid bus three hours north to Puerto Natales instead.

Formerly a remote, forgotten fishing village, it has grown into a dream destination for many an outdoor adventurer as the gateway to the infamous W Trek through the Torres del Paine National Park. Part of UNESCO's Biosphere Reserve programme, this park is probably the most beautiful in all of South America. It felt like a world away from the isolated quiet of Punta Arenas, with a steady stream of tourists dressed head to toe in North Face apparel, walking the paved streets with their shiny hiking poles, everywhere you looked. Most of the people I met on arrival were middle-aged, wealthy Americans who'd booked their guided trek many months earlier for many thousands of dollars. Their beds for each of the four nights they'd spend inside the park were reserved and probably included an electric blanket and a nice bottle of aged, room-temperature red wine on arrival to decompress from the day's walking.

My hopes of simply showing up and managing to start the trek in the next day or two began to feel more and more unattainable. Everywhere I inquired gave me a convoluted, contradictory tangle of instructions for booking my last-minute place, so I decided to go it alone and unguided – I hadn't come this far to give up. That afternoon I found a free information seminar in one of the hostels, set up to help people like me who couldn't afford the expensive tours and were hoping to risk the trail solo – but to do so, you needed some important knowledge. Primed with a notepad and pen, I became a sponge for every syllable spoken over the two-hour talk, and by the end of the following day I had run many rings around the small town to book my bus and boat to and from the trail and various camping grounds within the park, each of which I had to be able to walk the distance between in the light of a 12-hour day. I'd rented some equipment, bought more and arranged an impressive selection of snacks. It had been an infuriating hassle, but in the end it had only cost me a couple of hundred euro instead of a couple of thousand. Sitting in front of my hostel's open fire with a slice of pizza and a beer the night before my departure into the park, I felt proud of the most substantial return of my self-sufficiency yet and excited to take on arguably the world's most famous hiking trail. I was looking forward to seeing what merited the price tag so many people were willing to pay.

For five days straight, from the first break of morning light until nightfall, I walked largely in silence and alone amid one of the most remote and sublimely beautiful landscapes on the planet, crossing long bouncing suspension bridges hung high above the crisp, white surface of a creeping glacier, through deep green valleys surrounded by jagged snow-capped rock and past high panoramic lookouts, all culminating in a testing pre-sunrise ascent to the iconic Torres del Paine peaks. On the first day of my trek I met some other solo female travellers attempting the trail unguided too, and we formed a small, safe group and shared the path, chatting and exchanging stories, which allowed us to build our confidence in this wild, lonely place. The weather in Patagonia can be notoriously unpredictable and untamed, with extremes of temperature across the year and periods of intense wind and rain. Before meeting those girls, it had occurred to me that if I was to roll my ankle or have a fall, with only myself and my fully functioning legs to get me from A to B within a tight window of daylight, it could be a disaster, so it was incredibly comforting to have them nearby. But the days were long and, naturally, large distances fell between us along the route, leaving hours and hours of nothing more than steady, almost meditative walking and my own stream of useless, repetitive thoughts for company.

That was the first thing I really noticed, with only the whistle of the wind and the chirping of birds for distraction: left unchecked and to its own devices, my mind really did engage in a whole lot of useless, repetitive thinking. On average I walked about 25 kilometres a day while gaining and losing altitude along a path of varying quality and this generally took me between 7 and 11 hours, enough time to get well acquainted with the current state of my headspace, and the mindless stream of thoughts started to annoy me so much that I actively decided to think about something productive. At this point on my travels, I was aware that I had been living in an impoverished mental representation of my much fuller and more complicated self. That simply had to be true for me to have succumbed to the stress and anxiety brewing inside my own body with such surprise. How had I missed it? How had I run on empty for so long without knowing? Flaws are ubiquitous within the human condition, but why can we so often spot the vulnerabilities, weaknesses, self-serving biases, defences and coping mechanisms in others while remaining unaware of these in ourselves? Recognising this blind spot, I started to take an inventory of my life experiences and the effects they may have had on who I am, how I behave and the whole state of affairs that had brought me to this point.

I thought about my mam's seemingly endless and painful battles with her health throughout my youth and how much I had loathed helplessly watching her suffer. One vivid memory of this time came to mind over and over as I walked. When I was young I loved to draw and paint and I would regularly enter art pieces made with my mam's help for competitions in our local credit union or bookshop. On one occasion, I was making a Halloween-themed bookmark in the shape of Dracula in a coffin. I remembered sitting at my kitchen counter, colouring my entry with my hands shaking uncontrollably. My mam was bent over on all fours in severe pain, vomiting bile into a towel on the floor in the adjoining room as she tried to overcome another bout of gallstones wreaking havoc in her abdomen. Intermittently, as the pain would ease just enough, she would come to my side with enthusiastic praise and encouragement for the progress I'd made and, not knowing how else to help her, I would suppress the urge to cry out in fear and instead kept colouring, as if the quality of what I could produce was directly correlated to how well she would feel. I won that competition and I remember being overcome with a sense of guilt and shame that this was all I could offer in terms of help to my poor mam.

I was always petrified of losing her. She was my only source of constant, reliable love and care in this world. I felt a deep but precarious attachment to her and I knew that the uncertainty and helplessness of it had overwhelmed me at times, unable to cope with the reality that she might not win the next round. But it was only now that I started to make the obvious connection between these experiences and my own neurotic levels of hypochondria throughout my adult life, noticing how my anxiety had initially manifested as many elaborate illnesses, something I was deeply fearful of and thus the perfect feeding ground for it to take hold and spiral into disorder. I also considered how having my attachment to my only secure parent constantly under threat may have played a leading role in my subsequent choice of men and my pattern of dysfunction in forming healthy long-term romantic relationships, how it may explain why I only seemed to have access to two extreme ends of the spectrum: a very guarded, cold aloofness or an extremely dependent, hyper-concerned neediness. As this train of thought trickled on, I recalled that when I had been dating D I would have a terrifying recurring dream in which he died and I was certain I couldn't live without him. I would wake up crying hysterically every time it happened and cling to him like a koala for a day or two until the fright from the dream had passed. With every new and formerly unconnected association came another and another and another after that, like my brain had just woken up from a long slumber. It was becoming clear that I had been carrying these unacknowledged hurts and fears with me for a lifetime, projecting them into the world and shaping it within the limits of these expectations.

Wandering through the humbling expanse of the French Valley with a bright, cloudless blue sky providing the stark backdrop to a magnificent hanging glacier, which dominated the scenery with rumbles of distant avalanches as building-sized icebergs caved from its face, I felt a willingness to examine the uncomfortable aspects of myself here, considering how entirely insignificant I was. I thought about my relationship with my dad growing up and how I had been convinced it had had little to no effect on me as an adult. I had logged it in the recesses of my memory as a fairly underwhelming and commonplace father–daughter situation, a closed chapter of no real significance, until I had unwillingly happened upon some of its lasting influence with my therapist just before leaving home, and I hadn't really thought about it since. But perhaps not forming a relationship with my father for most of my childhood only for him to transform into the tyrannical figure of my adolescence and early adulthood had also had an effect on how I conducted myself in the world. I thought about having hated him with such intensity only to crave his love and acceptance to the same degree, if not more, and how much I'd despised relying on him while knowing I needed him nonetheless.

Our troubled and often explosive relationship had formed the basis of my understanding of men and how they should treat me. It had also given me my framework for handling and navigating conflicts of varying intensity, something that had been reinforced almost daily for many years. To say that I could see now that these important life lessons had been grossly misguided and internalised in an unhealthy, distorted manner was an understatement. My dad and I may have thankfully begun to rebuild our relationship with the love and respect it always deserved, but I understood now that these engrained examples and their resulting impulses wouldn't just disappear because of that privilege: I would have to work to rewire them.

With each passing hour of reflection, it became more and more apparent how destructive our broken parts can become if we do not assume the responsibility of, firstly, becoming aware of them and, secondly, working to heal them. When we know ourselves better, we can do better. When we can see what it is we lack, we can work to fill ourselves up. When we know what it is that has hurt us, made us angry, fearful or ashamed, we can become free from the unconscious grip of reaction and act out of conscious, considered choice. In that regard I had been asleep, running on automatic, for far too long.

Every night I crawled into the sleeping bag in my tent exhausted, my body aching and muscles tight. An old injury was starting to flare, inflaming my right knee and hip, and a new injury in my ankle was swelling so much that my hiking boot barely fit on that foot any more. I'd banged my toes on so many exposed roots, sharp rocks and unexpected steps that my nails were nearly all purple with the exception of a few lucky escapes. The simple act of walking was becoming difficult and painful, and as insightful as the introspection had been, I was, again, truly fucking sick of myself. But I'd read an Eckhart Tolle quote somewhere once, long before I'd needed it, which seemed to be appropriate now, a simple but brilliant analogy about growth and how it is achieved the same way, whether it's emotional or physical, comparing how we temporarily hurt and tear our muscles in the gym so that the fibres will heal stronger and more resilient. It was this small but meaningful metaphor that gave me the encouragement I needed to sit with my foot in a stream of freezing glacier water in the darkness of the early hours of the morning until it went completely numb and I could reapply my bandages, strap on my boot and keep walking, because I knew this wasn't really about the physical challenge: it was about the mental one it was facilitating.

Climbing slowly upwards under cover of night to watch the approaching sunrise paint the three symbolic peaks of Cordillera Paine a bright, blazing orange, I knew my time in the park was coming to an end so I forced myself to think just a little more. I had walked away from my career, my relationship, my home and nearly all of my possessions, and with that I'd lost the predictability of my future and a huge amount of my constructed sense of self on the threshold of my third decade, when most people are doing the polar opposite. It reminded me of a much larger and louder lesson, similar to the one I'd learned many years earlier when I'd lost my hair. Stripped back to basics, without the buffer of persona and all its external trimmings, I could see my authentic self without the decoration or the notion of who I aspired to be, and I suddenly felt incredibly embarrassed.

Up until that point, I don't remember feeling any real emotion regarding the many things I'd run through in my mind on those days spent silently walking. I'd been like a detached observer of my own story. But in these last moments of stillness spent taking in the overwhelming grandeur of Patagonia's most astounding natural wonder, a mental shutter went down. It had been five days of ruminating on who I am and why I am the way I am, trying to identify all the suffering that could have contributed to it, when in reality I had suffered so little that it could be argued that I barely knew what suffering was – all I had to do was look around me to verify that fact.

Real suffering was my mother meeting each new day of illness with such grace, or my cousin Kate's immediate family rebuilding their lives in the wake of her senseless loss, or tiny Magdalena from camp Bidi Bidi still offering that bright smile in the midst of devastation. My life had been nothing short of bubble-wrapped in comparison. It hadn't been any suffering that had ultimately caused me to fall victim to my mental health. It had been my own poor choices, my greed, ignorance and whatever else. It had been the consequences of my own actions and here I was wasting time allocating weight and value to the ordinary, underwhelming experiences of my life in search of a more profound answer. I felt like a drama queen, a spoiled first-world whinge bag. I was no philosopher – I was just an idiot.

So often during those years I took one step forward only to take two steps back.

CHAPTER 15

i stopped running

'Your task is not to seek for love,
but merely to seek and find all
the barriers within yourself that
you have built against it'

RUMI

Scratching past the shallow top layers of my existence brought feelings and versions of myself I didn't like to the surface, so after the W Trek in Patagonia, much like after the many bus journeys through Central America, I just stopped scratching and retreated to the safety of what was comfortable. It's difficult to portray the slow passing of this time in words, but for many months I didn't spend a single moment thinking about anything other than how best to fill my day. I returned to the default pattern that had always worked for me when things were uncertain: keeping busy and habitually distracted. From the town of Puerto Natales I travelled north through

Patagonia for a few more weeks, crossing the border into Argentina and trekking some of the endless hiking options around the beautiful village of El Chaltén, except this time I didn't allow any distance to fall between me and the people I met along the way, keeping a consistent companion on all the trails.

Having exhausted my reasonable options in Patagonia, I headed further north to reacquaint myself with the vibrant city of Buenos Aires before catching a ferry across the narrow Río de la Plata estuary that separates Argentina from Uruguay by just 50 kilometres. Starting in the picturesque UNESCO-protected and quite European-esque town of Colonia del Sacramento, I spent a couple of weeks beach-hopping along the sunny southern coastline of the country until I almost reached the coastal border of Brazil. One stop worth mentioning from this time is Cabo Polonio because it was without a doubt the most bizarre place I visited in all of South America. In Patagonia I'd befriended two Israeli guys who namechecked this small village as a worthy visit. 'If you end up in southern Uruguay, you have to make a stop in Cabo Polonio,' they'd told me as we sat engulfed in bean-bags in the common room of our hostel watching a grainy Spanish cartoon on an ancient telly. 'It's really something.' And that was where they had left it, neglecting to mention all its strange and magical details.

To get to Cabo Polonio I took a local bus from the very glamorous surrounds of Punta del Este, Uruguay's designer version of *Geordie Shore*, and was dropped off at the edge of a highway and directed towards what looked like a small closed visitors' centre with an empty car park. Confused, I 'signed in' and was then 'collected' by an enormous open-top double-decker monster truck. Its operator and I, the only passenger in this massive vehicle, traversed bumpily through dense forest and over large sand dunes for almost an hour to arrive at the most beautiful, untouched stretch of coastline you could ever imagine. Cabo Polonio's official population is 70, if you discount the large colony of sea lions that share the shoreline here, and the residents fight to maintain the village's completely removed, barefooted boho bubble. Wood, nails and hope hold the few ramshackle buildings in the area together, there is no mobile coverage or internet and a weak current of electricity is turned on for a short window during the day. There is one shop, which opens and shuts as it pleases, and no running water – they wash with water collected from wells or rainfall. It is a daily ritual to applaud the sunset. After dark the true magic of the village comes alive, as crackling bonfires are lit outside almost every residence and hundreds of candles and lanterns pierce the darkness. Someone with an out-of-tune guitar or a set of drums can always be heard giving a live performance in the distance, and for everything the area lacked, there seemed to be no shortage of Uruguayan red wine on offer. At another time, in another mindset, I could have decided to drop off the grid and move here indefinitely, but I just couldn't take the amount of space this place left free for thought and the lack of distractions. I had come to this tiny, remote stop hanging off the edge of a peninsula with intentions to stay for a week, but I only managed two nights before I had to escape on the giant monster truck back to civilisation.

Over the coming months it was much of the same rush as before. From Uruguay I backpacked through all of Paraguay, which was a consuming feat in itself, considering less than 20 per cent of the entire country's roads are paved. Once I finally reached the northern border I crossed east into Brazil via the thundering and truly staggering wonder that is the Iguazu Falls, the largest waterfall system on the planet. Then drawn back to the coast again, I slowly plotted my way further north from the beautiful surrounds of Florianópolis to those of Rio de Janeiro, with one particularly memorable coastal stop along this route being the paradise island of Ilha Grande. Formerly home to a leper colony and then to a high security prison housing all of Brazil's most notorious criminals, the island only opened to the public in 2004, and because of this unique history it has remained unspoiled and thus particularly special. But I mustn't have had my fill of underdeveloped, offbeat locations because from Rio I returned inland to explore the Amazon jungle for a bit, and in doing so I crossed another border, this time into Ecuador, where I eventually worked my way west as far as the country's capital, Quito, to catch a flight to the Galapagos Islands in the heart of the Pacific.

The Enchanted Islands, as they were formerly known, are home to the type of extraordinary biodiversity that inspired Darwin's theory of natural selection, and with the exception of one species of sea lion and one species of tortoise, the animals here, most found nowhere else on the planet, have never been hunted and so have never developed a fear of humans, affording visitors the opportunity to get unusually close to them in their natural habitat. The Galapagos is also home to a type of daisy that grows 20 metres tall, a pelican with a 7-foot wingspan, the smallest, cutest breed of sea lion on the planet and the only species of penguin found north of the equator.

I'm aware that this travel route is now tipping towards ridiculous, but I'm not done yet. Having ticked off almost every country in both Central and South America, with the exception of Venezuela, which was in the grips of a deep political crisis, and its difficult-to-reach neighbours, I decided it was now time to circumnavigate half the globe in search of an untapped source of novelty, so I booked a flight to Japan, opening up all the possibilities of a new continent.

And, honestly, I was having an absolute ball – until I just wasn't any more.

No one and nothing, not even this privileged existence spent doing little more than draining the hard-earned contents of my bank account, will satisfy us for long if we are not awake, aware and at peace within ourselves. Each new acquisition or accomplishment simply pushes out the goalposts of fulfilment, and it is a potentially lifelong race to an unreachable finish line. This only became obvious to me again when I arrived in Japan. I had spent the guts of the previous decade dreaming of visiting this place, putting off every opportunity that had presented itself until I felt the timing was perfect. It had to be cherry blossom season and I had to have enough time and money to explore the entire length of the country unrestricted. Here I was with my dream now a reality, yet I was haunted by an unrelenting hum of low-level anxiety and an intense exhaustion that ran deeper than the expected bout of jet lag.

We are cyclical creatures, bound to repeat our patterns. In Japan, while methodically clocking up stop after stop on my long-held wish list, I could no longer hide from the fact that I'd run myself down to empty again and all that had changed was the means through which I had done it. I would find myself at one of the incredible sights on my list and, instead of being in awe or full of gratitude for having finally made it there, I'd have a moment where I'd think, *I don't even care*. There had been a time when I'd craved these experiences with every cell in my body, so to find myself feeling any way indifferent had to mean there was something wrong. I'd reached my saturation point with novelty. I felt underwhelmed, drained and, frankly, sad.

Long-term travel is not easy, long-term travel alone is even more challenging, and I had been going hard at it for almost a year now. This unconventional and exciting lifestyle had become commonplace, no longer affording me the highs it once had, and I could feel that it would soon stop offering the respite it had given me from my feelings of anxiety and panic too. It was a veil, another buffer for the problem. Travelling could afford me the time and space to gain some self-awareness, but it was becoming clear now that a life spent on the road, flying by the seat of my pants, could not and would not be the ultimate solution. After many months of roaming I was in search of an answer once more, and after a little deliberation I felt a pull to return to the one activity I knew would reliably provoke the parts of me I probably needed to examine most.

I'd never harboured any deep desire, or any desire at all, for that matter, to become a yoga teacher, nor did I have anything more than the most fundamental skill set to pursue this notion, but I knew two things to be true: yoga is an age-old practice and a multibillion-dollar industry that offers more wisdom than I'd previously considered, before dismissing it as a stupid contortionist class for people who are kind of full of shit, and nothing in this world, outside of an argument with my dad growing up, had ever made me quite as physically enraged or hysterical as partaking in its practice. Outside of those four imprisoned days in Costa Rica, where yoga had been the only alternative to utter boredom and the lack of access to my phone, there was generally something in the movement, or the stillness, or the combination of the two that sparked my ugliest undisclosed emotions. My reaction to yoga just wasn't normal and I wanted to figure out why.

Motivated to research my options, I found a course taking place over four weeks in a retreat centre called Vikasa on the beautiful island of Koh Samui just off the east coast of Thailand. Since leaving home almost a year before, I hadn't spent more than six consecutive nights in the same dormitory bed, so the idea of having my own small room where I could unpack my battered backpack for a little while felt like an absolute luxury. On top of that, our days would be scheduled for us from start to finish, various types of restorative activities were mandatory and all our meals were included – I could literally wash my hands of the daily task of militant self-reliance while being kept suitably busy, and that, too, felt profoundly appealing. I was the most unlikely soon-to-be yoga teacher, but the decision felt so right it was almost unquestionable: I'd leave Osaka for Koh Samui.

On the flight, I thought about how it had been over a decade since I'd visited Thailand – it was nice to have finally cultivated the courage to return. This was the country that had given me my first lesson in real loss and sparked my true love of travel and nature. It felt appropriate and full circle, if a little like a Hollywood movie script, that this might be the place where I would finally find my peace.

I really had no idea what to expect from my teacher training, and that ignorance definitely served me well. If I knew then what I know now I'd have quickly hopped one island over to Koh Pha-ngan, ordered a cold Chang, put my feet up, said good riddance and waited it out for the carefree buzz of the next Full Moon Party. But in truth, from the very first minutes of our very first sunrise hatha vinyasa, I could tell I was in way over my head, and from then on the intensity did not wane whatsoever for the duration of our training. Every morning we did an almost three-hour-long yoga flow that included advanced breath work, far too many postures of varying discomfort held for longer than felt humanly possible, a deep guided meditation and, finally, my much-beloved savasana, which is where you just lie down. I was so overcome by the intensity of the wake-up call and the practice without even a sniff of a coffee that I fell asleep every morning without fail in this posture for the first couple of weeks. After the morning's training we'd take a short break for breakfast, which was followed by our daily four-hour bout of lectures with topics ranging from anatomy to yogic philosophy, followed by another short break for dinner, into a couple of hours of guided self-inquiry with the use of yin postures, mantras or mindfulness workshops, and then finally 90 minutes of meditation before calling it a night to get some much-needed rest so we could wake up and do it all again the next day.

There's a chance this schedule might sound enjoyable in writing, but let me tell you, my body has never ached like it did during the first two weeks of this training – even when I was doing nothing at all, it hurt just to be alive. If it weren't for the financial investment I'd made for the privilege, I'm not sure I'd have stuck it out. On a positive note, in the beginning I think my body and my mind were in too much shock to generate the emotional reaction yoga usually caused within me, so I didn't take much notice when our course instructor introduced us to our point of contact for when we needed 'to navigate the difficult feelings that will arise from this training'. This did, however, make me feel like less of a lunatic for having such a visceral reaction to the practice – maybe I wasn't alone.

The flooding of new movements and a new language to describe them had me running on autopilot simply trying to make it through the demands of each day without collapsing, until about halfway through the course I experienced the emotional jolt of a small personal upheaval. You might be wondering what happened to the man I'd ended up liking a lot more than I'd ever planned to in Peru. Well, we did meet again, many more times over many more months, and on each occasion he had grown to mean more to me than

I was probably ready for. In all the chaos of my life I no longer knew what my future would hold, but I had come to hope that, no matter what, it would include him, and that felt like an anchor in the storm. I was still far from perfect at navigating these new emotions, but for the first time ever I had managed to resist the urge to push love away. The vulnerability of it still sometimes caught me off guard and made me feel unnerved, but every day I asked myself to show up as my genuine self, flawed and authentic, instead of hiding behind the mask of a cool, dismissive independence. I began to share with him my weaknesses and my needs as best I could articulate them and finally allowed myself to admit that I deeply desired a partner to understand and overcome these things with. A partner to love me for me.

It was scary but necessary. Most of our hurt comes from our relationships, but so does most of our healing. When we feel safe in a soul-to-soul meeting we can often reveal the best and most beautiful parts of ourselves, and I started to think that maybe true freedom is being without anxiety about our imperfections. In finding this ability to surrender and trust, I also finally seemed to crack open a side of myself I'd never met before, a soft, patient, selfless love that I'd never been able to offer anyone before, and it felt incredible to take the risk and brave connection like this. Even on my worst days, my feelings for him propped me up, gave me a safe place to turn to for guidance, laughter or sometimes just an ear, and I loved being able to finally offer the same presence to someone in return.

In many ways, I wish I could tell you that this turned out to be the fairy tale I'd been waiting for, but what happened in reality may have been my greatest gift. Dave left my life just as suddenly and spectacularly as he had entered it. A whirlwind of passion and excitement was now just a memory, a scent on my pillow at the break of dawn. All hope of an imagined future disappeared in an instant and I was utterly crushed. He could never have known this, of course, but in executing his right to walk away, for his own reasons, he brought me face to face with my biggest fears of all: abandonment, rejection, not being good enough, to come as you are, to do the best you can and have it deemed unworthy. Whatever you want to label it, I had feared it so unreasonably my entire life that I had never let it be an option. My walls had always been up. Until

Dave, I would have compromised on anyone and anything to save myself from the potential pain, and I had. It was clear now that I had done the same to every man who'd ever tried to love me. I had abandoned them every day in small ways with my inability to open up, to be myself or communicate properly, until ultimately I'd abandoned them physically. I was always the one who left. In fact, I always kept one foot outside the door, primed and ready to flee. I was always the one in control. I was always playing tug-of-war for the masculine energy in the relationship, even though I desperately wanted to feel safe in being the opposite. The little voice inside my head screaming, 'Please hug me tight, tell me you love me and you're glad to be here with me, tell me everything is alright,' while on the outside I defiantly maintained my aloofness. Now there was nowhere to run, no work to be done, no drugs to take and no sights to see. I had somehow found myself in this inescapable collision of mindset and setting, and I had no choice but to fully weather the tsunami of emotion that followed the initial shock of this loss.

But before I could really feel the emotion, I had to give myself permission for the indulgence.

I had to allow myself to stop adding to the problem by feeling guilty for feeling how I felt. Raised in Ireland, the 'get over yourself' attitude had been instilled in me. We have little time for notions or nonsense, and I had always held myself to that cultural standard. Stop playing the victim, stop feeling sorry for yourself. You're grand. But in truth, I wasn't grand and I hadn't been grand in a long time. If I couldn't yet feel it, it was at least obvious in the dysfunction of my romantic relationships, the decline of my health and the many ways I chose to keep myself numb, distracted and without real, considered purpose or direction. To me, suffering had to be something that happened on an epic scale, otherwise it wasn't worthy of acknowledgment. Suffering was deep distress, pain, loss or hardship – an elusive experience that affected my parents' generation and those before them, but not something I had any right to claim I knew anything about in my privileged life. In finding myself again reduced to the foetal position, engulfed by what felt to me like a profound pain, I started to reconsider this stance on what suffering is and who is entitled to feel it.

Maybe suffering doesn't have to happen on an epic scale. Maybe it is simply a quiet awareness that we are being less than we are capable of being. Maybe it is living a life limited by socially imposed ideals, a life appeasing everyone else. Maybe it is a slow, steady simmering of dissatisfaction. Maybe it is the gap between our expectations and our reality. Maybe is it the abstract and unarticulated frustration of a general lack of purpose and meaning, or maybe it is the unconscious recognition that you are on autopilot, repeating your harmful patterns and in doing so hurting yourself and those around you. And just like boiling water softens a vegetable and hardens an egg, maybe the same experience will affect two people entirely differently, yet that doesn't diminish the truth of either. Suffering is a subjective reality that cannot be empirically defined or owned by anyone. What feels like suffering to you is suffering.

But I had spent so long refusing to suffer. Instead, I had propped up my unacknowledged lack and hurt with my image, my status, my persona, my attempts at relationships, my workload, my choice of drugs and every other external stimulus until my body had simply given up, and then I'd found a way to blindly do it all over again. I had been betraying myself and so I could no longer trust myself or the decisions I made, and with that had come the unstoppable rise of chronic panic and fear – a fairly natural reaction when, in truth, you're navigating the world half-asleep.

In the forced long practices of yoga and meditation and in the quiet loneliness of my small room at night I began to sift through the stagnant, repressed negative emotions I'd accumulated over my lifetime. It felt like taking off a mask and asking myself to look, with radical honesty, at the totality of who I was rather than just the bits that suited me and the story I'd created. Beyond the fear, there was so much more unexpressed feeling, inhibited anger, shame, humiliation, envy and guilt – a spiral of entangled mental tension. It is not within human nature to sit in these emotions for long periods. We hate them. We develop well-oiled, almost reflexive defences, phobias, social maps and deeply rooted self-regulation to avoid them at all costs. They make us cringe on recall and they rarely appear in the script of who we are. Yet they are there, to various degrees, in all of us. Everyone's life is marked with the stories of their own tragedies, whether they choose to deem them worthy of the weight they carry or not. We all act out of our own pain more often than we realise, and we all have unmet needs. I was just trying to no longer feel guilty for simply accepting these facts with regards to myself and deciding to do my best to heal them.

I think practising yoga at this time gave me the tools I needed to not run away from what felt like failure. Having arrived without any real prior experience, I learned quickly that for me yoga wouldn't be about holding the perfect posture: it would be about reaching for it, a sentiment I tried to incorporate into my thinking outside of training. To make the process more bearable, every day I would dedicate some time to reflecting on how far I'd come, how many fears I'd already conquered just to get there, and that gave me further encouragement to keep feeling deeper, to not be afraid of my authenticity. But ultimately, I think my greatest incentive was that I had to be able to live with myself – something I had clearly been finding increasingly difficult. When every transient thing, every thought, feeling and experience, arises and disappears as it always does, there is only me, and in the end if I do not truly understand, like and forgive myself, I can have no inner peace and, at its core, with any decoration peeled back, my future will look the same as my past.

I have always hated conflict. I would do anything to avoid it in favour of even a feigned harmony. But in avoiding it for so long, it seems I'd started a war within. I would have said I was someone who never got angry because I didn't scream or shout, but I was, in fact, someone who just didn't know how to express my natural and healthy feelings of anger. I thought anger was bad, so I pushed it down. In the discomfort of my physical training and the long hours spent sitting focused on my breath, I tried to allow myself to feel unconditionally and without judgement whatever emotions came up, and I was shocked by how much anger was inside me. It's difficult to admit, but I was angry with my mam for always being on the verge of leaving me with each new battle with illness. I was angry with my dad for his own emotional immaturity and lack of self-awareness, for allowing his unresolved pain to manifest as his own unrestrained anger, for taking no responsibility for that energy he expended into my young, impressionable world. I was angry with my cousin Kate for not running even five minutes late that morning, for not taking a different route to work, for not somehow spotting the sirens. Angry with every man who hadn't looked away when I was changing on a shoot, every man who'd taken a liberty when I was drunk, every man who'd made me feel devalued or discarded. But more than all of that combined, I was angry with myself, and one reason stood out light years ahead of the rest. I still hadn't fully faced the fact that an incredible man had also walked into my life, a strong and steady man, who had been tender and kind, built up my confidence, believed in me and respected me, and I had hurt him. I had to accept that and forgive myself for it. It wasn't personal – it's never personal – it was the unintentional projection of this anger I was discovering.

Still, I was ashamed of having behaved that way, and beneath that there was more shame. I was ashamed of many of the choices I'd made when I was young and under the influence, ashamed of having slept with my friend's boyfriend most of all, humiliated by the aftermath and the beating my reputation deservedly took – and there was more humiliation to be found too. Whether I wanted to admit it or not, I felt humiliated by the fact that almost everyone I knew was settling down, chosen and deemed good enough to partner with. But not me; I wasn't good enough. That made me envious, something I thought I had learned to recognise and overcome. For the first time, I could see that these repressed emotions were feeding into each other, a cycle of unexpressed, blind hurt that I now desperately wanted to end. I could see it, but I still had to figure out how to let it go. First, I decided that letting go wouldn't have to mean I no longer cared – instead, it would mean I accepted the past exactly as it was and would find peace with how things unfolded. In doing so, I hoped to disentangle my old patterns of behaviour that keep getting in the way of my happiness in the present.

Every day at the end of our self-inquiry class we would do something called a pentacle meditation. Lying on my back with my arms and legs stretched out like a star, I would breathe in deeply, focusing all my energy on my navel, curling my toes, tightening my fists and drawing all my muscles tightly towards the centre of my body – I would squirm with the tension. Then I'd release everything in one quick flood, my breath and my body relaxing instantly in a symbolic letting go, and the tears would quickly follow. Other days we would write down the things we needed to release from that day, from our past or even from our imagined future. We'd burn the words in a fire by the ocean and that also felt like letting go. I was starting to unbind from my own story, and in doing so I could truly resonate with the pain others felt, my poor dad's most notably. This growing clearer perspective was a great aid in finding genuine forgiveness. I was starting to make sense, understand, forgive and let go in unison. It felt like a large chunk of my ego died during this time, like I grew stronger and in doing so became inexplicably gentler. I had unpacked the recesses of my mind, examined what I found, accepted it as it was and decided I still liked myself, maybe more than I ever had, and no one can shake those roots once they start to grow.

I fell victim to my mental health for a number of reasons. Maybe I was partially susceptible, partially ignorant and partially contributing. But there was an important message for me hidden in the mess of that intolerable discomfort when I stopped running, dismissing and turning away. There was a time when I felt with conviction that my headspace was unrecoverable – that I was gone and I would never return. Nothing I've ever experienced, voluntarily or involuntarily, has brought me to the depths of fear quite like that time in my life. Yet even with that said, I would not change a moment of it – I wouldn't take it away given the chance. In fact, I dread to think who I would be without that experience. I take no credit for any growth I've found in light of it because it was forced on me – I wasn't wise enough to figure out I needed it on my own. But I could never resent the losses because I gained so much more. Beyond a passport full of stamps and a head full of memories, the welcome return of my clear skin, normal digestion and ability to sleep, it has given me a new level of tolerance and respect for my spectrum of negative emotions, the ones I used to deny existed inside me almost entirely, which in turn has resulted in a stability of mood I was never able to find before. After all that time spent introspecting, my sense of self has grown stronger, clearer, more defined and, as I mentioned, I like who I am now. And that is really an invaluable gift, one that has allowed me to recover the self-esteem I was lacking and thus the courage to finally respect and uphold my own boundaries, which in turn has restored that lost sense of trust in myself.

The whole experience has helped me to resonate and connect with others in a way I never could when I was wrapped up in my own confusion. It's given me a first-hand understanding of the complexity of people's behaviours and the many layers of a person's internal experience. In turn, that has afforded me, maybe most importantly, an ability to not take things too personally. People project onto the world the stories they're telling themselves – it's rarely anything to do with you. This time taught me to accept life's inevitable and recurring promise of setbacks, that things are not simply destined to turn out how we want them to, and even still, in those unexpected twists and turns, we can find a passion, pleasure and vitality that comes from surrendering to what is rather than resisting it in an attempt to worry into existence what we imagine should be.

If you had asked me a few years ago, before all of this happened, 'Do you like yourself? Do you know yourself? Can you sit quietly with yourself? Do you respect and take care of yourself?' I would have answered yes to every question. But in truth, it was a resounding no and it took me crumbling to pieces and leaving behind everything I'd ever known to figure that out. I was a model with no self-esteem. I was a radio presenter with a debilitating fear of public speaking. I was the most unlovable, unattainable girl whose deepest need was to be loved and accepted as I am. I was an over-confident, over-competent, over-productive person who was actually none of those things at all: I was pretending. This duality, this opposite behaviour, this outward performance of the things we lack, fear or dislike about ourselves most is called reaction formation, and my impulse to do this as a buffer for my weaknesses ran so deep I almost built my entire life around it. I was completely misaligned and no amount of cultivated external validation would ever afford me these mocked traits: real self-esteem, confidence and self-acceptance, an unshakable understanding of your boundaries and self-worth, a purpose and direction in the choices you make for yourself and your future. Those things are earned and nurtured internally – they cannot be faked.

I was always busy, my calendar was always full, yet, even if it was just the faintest whisper, I had always known that I was running on thin air but I'd decided to ignore it, to deal with my deficits another day. Now, with them all laid bare before me, the good and the bad, I felt I could integrate my self as a whole and move forward with real autonomy for the first time in my life.

° ° °

I wrote these bullet points to myself at the end of my yoga teacher training as a reminder of some of the things I'd learned during that time:

- Almost all people, almost all of the time, are doing their very best with where they are and what they know.
- Very little is personal – people mostly act out of their own pain and in accordance with their own complex internal narrative.
- There will come a day when this will all be gone. Perhaps sooner than you think. Enjoy the journey.
- It's important to get comfortable with being uncomfortable or life is going to be a real struggle. Yoga can help with that.
- If you act out of feelings of scarcity or believe 'if they succeed then I must fail', you are in direct misalignment with the laws of nature – there is infinite abundance and more than enough for everyone.

- Your life is always guiding you in small ways every day.
- Be intentional with attention and where your energy goes – are those things in alignment with the life you want?
- Take responsibility for the energy you put into the world every day, the energy you dump into other people's day – wherever possible, make it purposeful.
- To find meaning, dedicate yourself to a cause that's bigger than you.
- We can't always control what happens to us and things will not always go our way, but in every setback there is an opportunity to adjust our perspective, practise gratitude, find new opportunities and grow with grace.
- It is never a loss – it is a redirection.
- Our greatest hardships are usually a doorway to our most significant growth, and though it seems unbelievable now, there will come a day when you will look back and say you'd never change that time.
- Status anxiety is a real thing, but success should be individually defined and not

influenced by social pressures. Let go of what your life is supposed to look like. Not being in line with conventional benchmarks for success is OK. Doing your own thing your own way is OK. Scary, but OK.

- Fear is the biggest limitation on what we are capable of, and we are capable of so much more than we can even imagine. The stories we tell ourselves give us implicit limits or possibilities, so it's important to have a story that lets us be the fullest we can, a story that lets us risk and learn. Facing our fears is a lifelong journey.
- To love is a privilege and it's always worth the risk.
- Everything I've ever done, I've done myself. That is something to be proud of.
- Being highly agreeable is a nice way to please everyone, but saying no and setting healthy boundaries is a nicer way to please myself.
- Not everyone is going to like you and that is definitely OK once you're sure you like yourself.

CHAPTER 16

the skydive

'I have always been delighted at the prospect of a new day, a fresh try, one more start, with perhaps a bit of magic waiting somewhere behind the morning'

J. B. PRIESTLEY

My stomach is knotted so tight I can't eat, and even if I could I'm fairly certain the steady flooding of nerves throughout my body would immediately expel whatever made it in. I haven't slept properly in nights, jolted awake in a panic and damp with sweat from the terror playing out on repeat in my dreams. I'm sure I'm tired and hungry, but I don't feel either of those things. I feel alert, primed, ready for action. I feel like I need to sprint around a football field a couple of times to dispel the effects of this horrible anticipation. We've had our safety briefing – 'If the parachute doesn't open, then …' and 'When the door is pulled back, I'll need you to look down and step out onto the wheel of the plane ...' OK, no problem. Disregarding the implicit message of certain death in the first sentence, you want me to get myself to that point by leaning out of the open door of an airplane flying at 14,000 feet, casually look down and then maintain a level of control over my body that allows me to step out with enough co-ordination to land my foot on a narrow ledge while 80-mile-per-hour winds force against my best efforts?

I've been thinking about that manoeuvre for over an hour now as we impatiently wait for the weather to reach optimum conditions for the jump. Every passing minute is torturous. The build-up, the places your mind takes you, the stories you tell yourself, that's the worst part. The anticipation. The expectation. The trying to imagine what it will be like. The fear is almost unbearable. Why am I doing this? I could just walk out the door, forget about it and get on with my life, maybe go for brunch and a coffee instead. If you had asked me a couple of years ago if I would ever do a skydive, I would have sworn no, not in this lifetime, not for any amount of money. If you'd asked me if I would like to be able to get past the fear to experience what it feels like to free-fall for 40 seconds, I would have said yes, but the first part was simply inconceivable. Daily confrontations with fear had become a real practice for me now and this would be my ultimate physical hurdle, the acid test for how much I'd changed and how much control I'd gained over my most potent and disabling emotions. I did want to experience a skydive, but I couldn't do it – that had been the story I'd always told myself. There's no way. I'd pass out, vomit mid-air, wet myself, perhaps die from the overwhelming fear and shock of it all, and that was, of course, only if my parachute actually opened – it was obvious that I would be one of the unlucky minuscule percentage of skydivers whose two parachutes tragically fail. That's what my head told me, over and over.

The palms of my hands and the soles of my feet are wet with sweat and the little stress twitch I get in my right eye is off. 'You're up, let's go!' I can't do this. Harnesses on, I can't do this. Another short briefing, none of it registered, I can't do this. As we walk across the runway tarmac I tell myself over and over to surrender to what is because this is happening no matter how intense the fear gets. If I pass out, I pass out, if I vomit, I vomit, but I'm jumping out of this plane regardless, so it's time to make the best of it. I almost can't believe it when I manage to get myself inside the plane, every cell in my body screaming to bail on this totally unnecessary endeavour. I can physically feel the urge to run away from this. But once the airplane door is closed, a strange thing happens: I completely relax, an unnerving sort of ease comes over me and I wonder if this is what dying feels like.

Suddenly, we're up to the jump height and the plane door opens. I've never been in a plane with the door open before: it's terrifying. I go first – I have to. If I watch someone fall into oblivion before me, I will spiral into the hysteria I am currently just about managing. The man strapped tightly to my back shuffles me to the edge of the opening. My eyes are clenched shut, any thoughts racing through my mind muddled by the howl of the wind – it is a force of sound and sensation I've never experienced before. '*Look down, step out, go!*' His yell is muffled and distant over the bellow, even though his mouth is at the opening of my ear. My breath is short and shallow, like a gasp that stops high in my chest, leaving me unsatisfied and increasingly dizzy. I take a long, deep inhalation through my nose and slowly, steadily exhale. '*Step out, go!*' he yells again. There is no other way out of this, I tell myself; falling is the only option. I open my eyes and look down. We're so high my brain can't even register what it should see as imminent death – it's so unreal it's actually not that scary. I stretch my leg out. The wind pushes it back and shakes it like a rag doll. It looks like something that doesn't belong to me. The man on my back keeps us steadfast with his experienced hold on the doorframe. '*Put your foot on the ledge!*' I keep my eyes focused on that ledge and nothing else, and once my foot lands safely and we've cleared the obstacle of the wheel, the man on my back flings us both into the open air with force, not affording me another nanosecond to contemplate the inevitable. I had tried to imagine this exact moment so many times – the sickening drop, the free fall, the utter terror of it: there's no way I'd open my eyes. None of that story is the reality. There is no drop, no sick feeling. My eyes are wide open. I am flying. There is no fear. I have finally learned to accept and push past the overwhelming symptoms of it. It is no longer controlling me. I have stopped fearing fear.

I am falling and it is bliss.

o o o

My relationship with fear is ongoing, of course, a life's work, ever evolving. At 31, I decided it was time to come home, to go back to college as a mature student and study for a degree in psychotherapy and counselling, to believe in my own capacity to eventually help others who succumb to the pressures of modern living just as I did. Making that decision to start over was scary. Facing the triggers and loose ends I'd left behind me in such a rush was scarier. My life now is a slow, steady and considered invested effort in comparison to the unruly array of impulses it was before, and writing this book was a deliberate choice – but that didn't make it any less petrifying. However, having your story witnessed is incredibly healing, so thank you for witnessing mine. It is nowhere near the worst, but it is my story nonetheless, and I decided to tell it to hopefully make a small contribution to the important conversation happening now around mental health.

I often hear people discussing its seemingly sudden prevalence in society as something of a 'bandwagon', but I believe it is, in fact, the malady of our time, born of too much privilege, too much choice, too many ways to 'fix' or mask the problems in our ever-more-complex lives. Every century, every generation has their burden: mental health (and the environment) is ours. And while you could argue it is a lesser evil compared with the bubonic plague or the fallout from a world war, that still wouldn't make it any less real or rife. It is, thankfully, becoming acceptable and even encouraged to openly discuss our bad days and our tough times, to ask for help and to lean on others when we need it.

But what is still rare to see is an honest conversation about the uncomfortable, awkward, embarrassing or socially taboo feelings and events that underpin these issues. It is in facing those things that our true healing can unfold and life can take on a new reality, free from the pain of our past or the constant management of the symptoms of our hurt. Beneath the consuming fear and panic of my anxiety disorder, exasperated by my meaningless workload, questionable lifestyle choices and general disregard for self-care or self-awareness, I found anger and other suppressed emotions, attachment issues and a quiet but relentless critic inside my head. The panic attacks and the destabilising effect they had on my life offered a gateway to change and transformation. They were heralding the possibility of something new and more authentic, and for that I'm now very grateful.

I've certainly grown and changed, but I'm far from having it all figured out – if anything, those years only highlighted for me how little I really know. The difference is that now I'm softer, kinder when I speak to myself, more open, more humble and more willing and eager to learn than I ever was before.

my practical tools for anxiety

I've collected some personal and practical notes on how I handled and continue to handle my anxiety here, which may be of interest to those reading this who are in the midst of their own battles.

I think it's important to point out, though, that there was never a point I 'got over' my anxiety – it still lives with me, and always will in some form or another, but I have established a very different relationship with it now. I have changed my perception of what it is – a natural feature of human life – and what it means when it arises in me – definitely not some kind of potentially harmful, painfully relentless, erratic demon that comes to inhabit my body against my will. First, I recognise, understand and respect the feeling, allowing it to be in all of its often distressing discomfort, and instead of spiralling down a rabbit hole of unreasonable explanations, catastrophic thinking, intense resistance or disassociation for relief, I try to stop, breathe, listen, consider and make alterations in the knowledge that it's for my own wellbeing. I try to view anxiety as my protector, as a tiny angel on my shoulder indicating from within when I'm not living authentically in the world, as something positive to be integrated instead of something menacing to be eradicated as quickly as possible.

o o o

ACTIONS TO TAKE IN THE MOMENT

1. In the beginning stages of physical symptoms (rapid heartbeat, sweaty extremities, brain fog, dry mouth, blurred vision), focus on exhalation. Elongating the exhalation to make it longer than the inhalation is the simplest and most effective way to calm the sympathetic nervous system. Our nervous systems still operate exactly as they did

many thousands of years ago. In nature, when we are under threat our breath becomes short and rapid, caught high in our chest. When we are relaxed or sleeping our exhalation naturally falls longer than our inhalation, so doing this voluntarily and with attention overrides the body's fight-or-flight response. Breathe in for a count of four and out for a count of six. Do this for 30 rounds. After that, assess how your body feels. If necessary do 30 more, this time focusing on progressive muscle relaxation throughout your body alongside the breath – relax your jaw, let your tongue fall away from the roof of your mouth, drop your shoulders away from your ears.

2. A panic attack can be defined as the loss of linear rationality – your more primitive brain stem hijacks the higher executive function of your prefrontal cortex and convinces you beyond reason that you are doomed: 'there is no hope of coming back from this' or 'this is just who I am' or 'this is how things will always be'. It is this underlying certainty of the loss of control that facilitates the spiral into unmitigated panic, an impulse so powerful it can even override our most deeply engrained need to conform to social norms and

avoid social judgement (meaning our bodies can betray us and freak out in public, adding humiliation to the long list of other horrible symptoms). To find a sense of control in these situations, use cognitive behavioural therapy tools, which are a powerful (but short-term) solution. Ground yourself by telling yourself your own story: 'My name is X, I was born on X date, I live at X address, my family's names are X, I go to school/work in X' and so on. This logical semantic thinking forces you to use your prefrontal cortex, which restores a sense of lost rationality. To further ground the mind, become aware of your surroundings: name the things you can see, name the things you can hear, name the smells, name the feelings. Ground yourself in your senses and bring your mind back to the present moment. Once you feel the panic begin to subside, use the breathwork technique above to continue de-escalating the nervous system.

3. If you are in an appropriate place or have headphones, please use these meditations composed by the Stress Management Institute of Ireland, in particular the chimes meditation: https://soundcloud.com/resilience-international. The studies conducted on these pieces of material are so

robust that the institute has made them available and free for public use.

◦ ◦ ◦

DAY TO DAY

1. The most effective action I took to overcome my anxiety was to study it thoroughly. Having a clear understanding of the neural and biological processes at work within my body meant the physical manifestations of those processes no longer scared me. I could talk myself through what was happening and give myself back that sense of control that anxiety and panic completely eradicate. A good place to start is with the book *Owning It* by Caroline Foran.

2. On a physiological level, you can influence anxiety through a few considered steps. The vagus nerve, which runs from the brain to the gut, is increasingly understood to be a primary component of wellbeing. Gut issues need to be addressed by a medical professional and treated properly – a probiotic is not a universal answer (for instance, if SIBO, the most common small

intestine bacterial overgrowth, is the cause of your digestive issues, a probiotic will make everything much worse). Gut problems and mental health problems are often intrinsically linked, so it's important to take proactive care of your gut health. Dr Michael Ruscio's book *Healthy Gut, Healthy You* is an accessible resource to gain an understanding of how to care for your gut. Daily supplementation with zinc, magnesium, vitamin D and vitamin B12 is important if you suffer from anxiety, as a deficiency in any of these can manifest with similar symptoms to anxiety or contribute to its emergence if you're already overtaxed or predisposed. Finally, issues with the thyroid and liver function also share the full symptoms list with anxiety. To rule these out as underlying causes, you'll need a full, fasted blood test. This is, of course, all personal choice and based on my own experiences, but it is useful for anyone struggling with anxiety to know that it may be rooted in or exacerbated by physiological causes that are often overlooked.

3. Keep a panic diary – over time this will allow you to identify patterns and triggers, which can be helpful in gaining a broader understanding

of what underlies your anxiety. It is also a useful bank of information to bring to talk therapy. Here is a simple panic diary template.

Date:
Level (0–10):
Time began:
Time ended:
Symptoms:
Where are you?
What were you doing when the attack began?
Are you alone (if not, list who is present)?
What were you thinking before the attack?
What were you thinking during the attack?
How did you talk back to the fears?
What actions did you take to calm yourself?
How did the attack end?
How would you respond differently next time?

4. Don't be disheartened by regressions or the feeling of a lack of progress. To arrive at a point where anxiety and/or panic is interfering with normal living or in need of treatment, your nervous system has most likely been running on an imbalance for quite some time – possibly simmering at all times, rarely or never switching

into rest and relaxation mode. This becomes your body's 'new normal' and sometimes people find the feeling of relaxation so alien that it's distressing. Stick with this process. It is slow but, like training a muscle every day, it will grow stronger incrementally and it is incredibly important work, especially on the good days when you feel you don't need to do it. Every single day, find a way to switch off your sympathetic nervous system (the fight-or-flight response) and activate your parasympathetic nervous system (the rest-and-digest response). It doesn't matter what form that takes: massage, acupuncture, meditation, yoga, flotation tank, reflexology – whatever floats your boat, but most importantly, whatever relaxes your body for 20 minutes every day. Stress is cumulative; relaxation, unfortunately, is not. Activating your parasympathetic nervous system needs to become a daily exercise, but once you've mastered it, the benefits for your overall wellbeing and managing your levels of daily anxiety are truly invaluable.

○ ○ ○

LONG-TERM SOLUTIONS

1. As above, activate the parasympathetic nervous system for at least 20 minutes daily.

2. Severe anxiety or panic is rarely an episodic event. It is the internal and external manifestation of underlying root causes or stressors. It may only break into conscious awareness during times of increased life stress, but it is there, in an unbalanced nervous system, at other times too. To untangle these (often unconscious) causes, talk therapy, like psychotherapy, is a great asset alongside the daily management offered by cognitive behavioural theraphy (CBT). CBT alone will only ever manage the problem, but getting to the root of the issue and resolving it empowers a person enormously in terms of self-awareness, self-acceptance and overall autonomy. I believe anxiety, as a debilitating issue, cannot exist in the face of autonomy, as its major prerequisite is a sense of the loss of control.

ACKNOWLEDGEMENTS

To every person mentioned in this book, those who have touched my life and contributed to making me who I am today, thank you – I hope I managed to tell my story without trespassing too much on yours.

To my family, most notably my dad, thank you for your endless love, support and encouragement, as well as your admirable courage and authenticity. I would be nowhere without you and I love you with all my heart.

To my friends, thank you for every reassuring call and text while I lived solely inside the bubble of my own head for months on end. Thank you for dropping around for tea, the evening walks and the hype on the days when I wanted to burn it all.

To Dave, thank you for believing I could, pushing me to find a publisher and always keeping an eye peeled for typos.

To Faith and Sarah, thank you for taking a shot on a first-time author with a partial manuscript; this book is one of the proudest accomplishments of my life, and it would never have been possible without you both.

To the powerhouse of girls at Gill – Aoibheann, Teresa, Ellen – and to Emma and everyone else who helped to make this idea into a reality, thank you. I have adored every minute of the process. It's been a privilege to work with you.

And lastly, to you, the reader – if you're still reading – thank you so much for choosing to pick up my book and give it your time. I am forever grateful.